LOVE IN A
DIFFERENT CLIMATE

LOVE IN A DIFFERENT CLIMATE

Men who have sex with men in India

jeremy seabrook

VERSO

London • New York

First published by Verso 1999
© Jeremy Seabrook 1999
All rights reserved

Verso
UK: 6 Meard Street, London W1V 3HR
US: 180 Varick Street, New York, NY 10014–4606

Verso is the imprint of New Left Books

ISBN 1–85984–837–0

British Library Cataloguing in Publication Data
A catalogue record for this book is available from the British Library

Library of Congress Cataloging-in-Publication Data
A catalog record for this book is available from the Library of Congress

Typeset by SetSystems Ltd, Saffron Walden, Essex
Printed by Biddles Ltd, Guildford and King's Lynn

[13618]

Foreword

Men who have sex with men (MSM) is a group that has always been hidden within Indian society, and a behavioural practice that is little acknowledged or described. On the few occasions when it is discussed or written about, it seems to be used interchangeably with homosexuality. This is an anomaly that, in India, is going to cost us dear in terms of planning sexual health interventions or bringing about sustained behaviour change in the times of HIV/AIDS.

I think it is important that people understand the difference between a gay identity and MSM behaviour. Often gay men want to highlight the gay agenda – which is necessary and essential – but in the Indian context we have to acknowledge that there is another reality. We have to find ways to empower MSM, not only for themselves, but also for the impact their behaviour has on women. This often means questioning the very premises on which our culture's values are based: our views of ourselves as individuals and as sexual beings; the institution of marriage; the status of women, children and young people.

MSM behaviour is implicitly accepted though taboo in Indian society. I have often heard women say, 'Of course men have sex with men, but this changes after marriage' or 'Yes, this exists, but my husband is not like that.' It is not uncommon for men to talk about male-to-male sexual behaviour as *masti* (fun) rather than as a sexual encounter. Young males are often seen as a gender by themselves, and therefore available for the pleasure of older men.

This book by Jeremy Seabrook, which details MSM practice in

Delhi, will go a long way towards shedding light and dispelling myths. It is actually the first book of its kind about MSM in India and will serve as a revelation to many. It is also a major step for advocacy on the issue.

Anjali Gopalan
Executive Director of the NAZ Foundation (India) Trust
June 1998

Acknowledgements

I am grateful to the many friends and colleagues who have helped in the making of this book.

First of all, I would like to thank Charu and Mukul in New Delhi and Dr Hari Dev Sharma of the Nehru Memorial Museum and Library for setting up a seminar at which I was able to hear the critical comments of academics and activists working in the area of sexuality in India. I am also indebted to Jude Howell and Sarah White of the Overseas Development Group at the University of East Anglia in Norwich, and to Linda Etchart of the London School of Economics. Special thanks to Jeffrey Weeks for his constructive critical support, and useful suggestions.

I owe much to Shivananda Khan of the NAZ Foundation in London for his insights into the issue of men who have sex with men in South Asia.

I am grateful to Group-Captain and Mrs Gopalan in Gulmohar Park, where I stayed while doing the research, and my special thanks to Anjali Gopalan and the staff at NAZ for being so free and open with their discussions. I should like to thank the men staffing the Humrahi Helpline and the Gay Men's Support Group in New Delhi. Thanks also to the AIDS Bhedbhav Virodh movement, especially to Sister Shalini and Ashwini Ailawadi, who first alerted me to the importance of these issues.

Thanks above all to all the men who shared their stories with me with such frankness and friendliness. I have concealed identities and blurred the outlines of their lives, in order to preserve anonymity; but the substance of what I learned remains.

Love and gratitude, as always, to Derek Hooper, for his continuing affection and support.

Jeremy Seabrook
London, April 1998

Introduction

During 1997 I spoke with seventy-five men who have sex with men in Delhi. I say 'spoke with' rather than interviewed because that is a far more accurate description of the encounters. In fact, I met many others – at least forty – but with the seventy-five whose lives are in some measure represented here, I had one or more conversations of some length. More than two-thirds of the meetings took place in the cruising ground which I will refer to as 'the Park'. This is open every day during daylight hours, and there are always scores of men there, walking, sitting, relaxing, meeting friends, picking up partners.

This circumstance alone makes it a unique site. It does not have the furtive quality of most cruising grounds for men who have sex with other men. It is open and light, and I encountered great warmth and friendliness there. I do not know of any place quite like it, either in Asia or in Europe. It was free of the tensions that characterise its equivalents in Europe, and it seemed to me that people responded to each other as people, prepared to talk, to exchange and compare experiences, even when they did not regard one another as prospective sexual partners.

Men who have sex with men: the expression is critical, because in India – as in many other cultures in Asia and Africa – concepts of being gay, or bi-sexual are not applicable to such relationships. It is in order to avoid projecting Western preconceptions onto other cultures and other ways of structuring same-sex contact that the more neutral term is used. It is very easy for the West, with its dominance of the cultural as well as the economic arena, to re-interpret the whole world in its own image and on its own terms. In this sense, even ideas of 'gay liberation' serve not as emancipatory slogans, but as new forms of colonialism and vehicles of control.

I am not claiming that the stories of the people I met provide a representative sample. For one thing, as a conspicuous foreigner (white as well), a mature gay man, I cannot pretend that my identity did not influence the nature and content of the discussions I had. These factors were not, however, necessarily wholly disadvantageous. I certainly aroused considerable curiosity which scarcely diminished when it became clear that I did not visit the Park for sex. 'What's he doing then?' they asked, when I was ensconced there every day, sitting, waiting, talking.

Not being young was a far smaller handicap than it would have been in the Western gay world. Many young men said that they cannot speak to their fathers about things that trouble them, particularly in the realm of sexuality and feelings; and they were keen to speak to someone older who might stand – however briefly – *in loco parentis.* This is in itself a significant comment, both upon the authoritarian nature of the family in India, and equally upon the hierarchies of youth and beauty which govern much of social intercourse in the gay world of the West.

As a European, I became the focus of some curious fantasies, since many people have heard that Europeans are far more open about sex than most Indians. Men wanted to know about sex in Europe and eagerly quizzed me as though I were an expert on blue films and kinky sex. Many must have been disappointed.

Being white is still widely considered to be a desirable attribute, the racism of the Raj having been deeply internalised by many people in the subcontinent. Although I always challenged such views, I was nevertheless the recipient of many confidences and advances that would not have taken place if I had been Indian: to be the beneficiary of racism while at the same time repudiating it vigorously is a curious kind of advantage, at times confusing and disorienting.

Further, being foreign had one other significant benefit for me. I was seen as a safe person to talk to, since it was clear that I was only a visitor to Delhi. Many men obviously felt they could entrust the expression of their feelings to someone who was only passing through and who would be unlikely ever to meet the people they were talking about. An exchange without consequences or repercussions; although, in fact, I have made a number of lasting friendships there.

Speaking Hindi had obvious advantages, and gave me access to conversations that would have been severely limited if I had spoken only English. The discovery that I could understand it told in my favour and doubtless led to a greater frankness than I might otherwise have anticipated.

Indeed, the whole experience was to confound and relativise many of the assumptions I have held for years as an out gay man in Britain.

Then there is the question of the Park itself. By definition, those who frequent it are self-selecting: by doing so, they become known to others and are compelled into some form of self-recognition, even though many still feel shame and anxiety about their sexual needs. Indeed, it is precisely through the accounts they gave of themselves – even when they were not wholly to be believed – that contemporary Indian attitudes to sex in general, and to men who have sex with men in particular, revealed themselves.

Yet how can one park in the capital city reveal anything about India as a whole? It is a commonplace that at least three quarters of the people of India still live in villages and that the cities – especially the great metropolitan cities – are in every way atypical of India. I was surprised to discover that among the men who frequent the Park, the map of India is more or less completely represented. The great social upheavals, the migrations and movements of the people of India may be read in the places of origin of those whose stories I heard: migrant workers; people who had left their families in the villages; people forced to flee unproductive land or landlessness; those moving in the service of big industrial companies; young men looking for a better life; opportunists; teenage runaways. The rural experience springs to life in the stories the men tell. Delhi has served as a place of hope and refuge for hundreds of thousands of people; just as its promises have failed as many others who, disappointed and rejected, have had to make some kind of accommodation with an unchosen – and often irreversible – migration to the city. These vast displacements of people are reflected in the relatively small number of men born in Delhi itself. I could not possibly have afforded to travel all over India; so I did the next best thing, which was to visit a place to which all of India comes.

One of the most difficult questions is, how do those who come to the Park reflect the wider experience of men who have sex with men in India? Many affirmed solemnly that such things do not happen in Madras or Nagpur or wherever they come from. Some state categorically that it is unknown in the villages. Most want to dissociate their place of origin from Delhi; somehow the native place must remain untainted by what they see as an aberration; and many want to preserve an image of a wholesome and sweet home, where wives, families and children remain, which is not contaminated by association with activities that still inspire shame and revulsion in many Indians.

In order to make sense of my own experience, I had to depend upon those who have studied the question more thoroughly. Although there has been much newspaper reporting in India on gays and homosex in recent years, most of this is both prurient and ill-informed. Surprisingly little research has been done.

The most useful comparative account of men who have sex with men came from a more practical source: the workers in the sexual health project of the NAZ Foundation have a more ample understanding than most others, since they develop and implement practical programmes to limit the spread of HIV in India. Through the work of NAZ in other parts of India, I was able to evaluate the stories and sexual histories I learned in Delhi. The staff have worked in rural areas, in small towns and in city slums and bustees; with their help and after considerable discussion with them, I was able to gain some insight into precisely which groups the Park attracts and which ones avoid it.

The only comparison I was able to make was with a similar project in Dhaka in Bangladesh. There, although they differentiate between male-identified and female-identified men who have sex with men, the pattern is similar. Men who penetrate others do not see the gender of the object of their sexual desire as having any significant implications for their sexual identity; whereas those who are penetrated call their partners *panthi* in Dhaka – a term which the *panthis* never apply to themselves. Those who are penetrated refer to themselves as *khotis*, as in Delhi. Certainly, the experience of Bangladesh confirms that of India: the great majority of men who have sex with men do not, on the whole, identify with Western cultural normals of being gay or bisexual. To impose such categories – except upon a small minority who have been much influenced by Western gay experience – is to bring alien concepts to the people involved; it is arrogant and disregarding of other cultures; and far from the respect for pluralism and diversity which the West now claims as one of its most characteristic attributes.

Some gay-identified men do come to the Park, although these are rather few. Similarly, there are factory workers, garment workers, even rickshaw drivers, although on balance the very poor are not represented in anything like their proportion in the population. In any case, the poor, especially young men in slums and in the villages, simply do it, they do not talk about it, name it or rationalise it. It is *maaza, masti, ananda karna*; it is fun, it is the kind of play or fooling around which is expected of young males. It does not need to be classified. The same is true with more mature men in the slums: some will have sex with younger men and boys, and it will not be discussed. The readiness with which men sleep together – usually for lack of space – permits a great deal of informal and opportunistic sexual contact. Often neither man involved will comment on what happened afterwards. Sometimes, if asked, they may say, 'It happened in sleep', which is perhaps the most extreme form of the elsewhere, in which things can happen that do not occur in daily life. In fact, in many of the stories the men told, the idea of sex happening in sleep or in dreams was a recurring metaphor.

On the other hand, the openly gay, the sons of privilege, tend to meet in the more up-market areas, at parties and in each other's houses. They are likely to be more discreet; and although some of their families may know and accept their sexual orientation, many will still maintain a careful concealment and, publicly at least, live out a life of impeccable heterosexual orthodoxy.

The social status of the men who visit the Park is fairly clearly defined; and this is important for the focus of this book. Most appear to be somewhere on the borderline of traditional Indian society, on the threshold of the modernising, liberalising shift which has accelerated in the past few years. This means that neither the very rich nor the very poor are among the principal visitors to the Park, although there are some remarkable examples of both. For the most part, they are workers, lower- and middle-class, white-collar workers and small businessmen. Their migrant status, their relative youth, their exposure to Western influences make them people in transition: a culture of becoming, in which the lineaments of their future are not quite clear, although those of their background, from which they are emerging, are overwhelmingly present. We are in the presence of a certain forming of consciousness, a kind of awakening, a different sense of being from that governed by casteism, communalism and the ancient hierarchies of traditional India. The politics of identity it most emphatically is not; but spaces are opening up, and being forced open, by the urgency of desires that can no longer be suppressed in secrecy and denial.

The most glaring absence in the stories of the lives recorded here is the woman's voice – the perspective of wives, mothers, sisters, daughters, aunts, cousins, friends. This is, perhaps, not surprising, since the whole reason for coming to the Park is to find men – for sex, friendship, affection, love; for release, comfort, reassurance; moments of tenderness as well as of quite brutal and functional discharge.

Yet the more I spoke with the men, and the more I determined to ask them about the women in their lives, the more disturbed I became by the bleak picture that emerged, blurred, indistinct and incomplete though it was. Even when they were denying that their sexual adventures caused grief or anguish to women, it was impossible to escape an overwhelming sense of the powerlessness, the intuitive knowledge, the anxiety and self-blame of women confronted by men who are emotionally absent, who are not completely with their spouses in the way that their wives must be with and for them. The nature of marital subservience became more clear than in any academic account I've ever read: women waiting for their husbands, the consolations of children and family often quite savourless, as they confront the hours of emptiness and ignorance. Are their days filled with poisoned wondering and speculation? Do they feel his absences as an avoidance, a revulsion, his delays as a comment on their own desirability? Do they prepare some favourite food, seek to make themselves more alluring, think up stories and amusing things that will delight him when he returns? Or does their role in the family protect them from doubt? Do they gain a sense of security from the indissolubility of family ties – acknowledged by virtually all the men also – which saves them from falling into sombre anxieties about what their husbands may be doing? When I voiced these feelings at a seminar in Delhi, one woman said, 'Perhaps they are simply relieved that their husbands are sparing them their attentions.' Such a possibility had not occurred to me.

Maybe, I suggested to one man, they also have relationships with other men, even with other women. He was genuinely shocked: 'You cannot even think of such a thing. Where would she go? How would she meet another man?' As for meeting other women, he said he was certain that such things never happen in India.

I obtained a revealing insight one evening at a discussion among a group of privileged, gay-identified – and mainly young – men about marriage. Most agreed that they would eventually marry, although three out of about fifteen said they would not. Of those who expected

7

to fulfil their family duty, the discussion focused on whether or not they would be able to do what was expected of them sexually. 'Will I be able to perform?' 'Shall I be able to give her what she wants?' The speculation concentrated on this: can we produce children, so that the family line is continued, social obligations are fulfilled and conventions observed. At no point were the feelings of the wife an issue. At last I asked, 'Where are the women in all this?' There was a moment of silence. 'But she doesn't have to do anything,' was the response. 'We are the ones who have to act. She only has to lie there.'

The questions that this book seeks to investigate were inspired by the work of NAZ, a sexual health project based in south Delhi which concerns both women and men. Its main concern is to prevent the spread of HIV, and NAZ works with female and male sex workers, with street children, in slums and hospitals. The workers learned by experience that the use of Western models of being gay simply did not reach those among whom they were seeking to promote safe sex. The insights they have achieved arose from direct and daily contact, from the need to discover, to react appropriately, to define what has remained obscure in India. I have benefited enormously from their understanding and wisdom, and it is on the foundation of their work that this book has been constructed.

Love in a Different Climate

I   WHO ARE THEY?

1. Age

20 and under:	11
21–30:	40
31–40:	16
41–50:	6
51–60:	2
Total:	75

It is perhaps only to be expected that cruising in the Park is an activity predominantly performed by young men. This is partly because traditional constraints on sex in India have denied many older men expression of same-sex relationships, and partly because public openness about such relationships is a recent development. This is, naturally, to the advantage of a younger generation.

One notable aspect of such relationships is that they are relatively less preoccupied with youth than their Western equivalents. The clearly demarcated peer groups in the West, which have evolved as the consumer society has become more sharply segmented, are less in evidence in India. This is not to say that young and attractive men are not more in demand than older men, but simply that contact between the generations still remains a powerful and living force. This is, in part, a reflection of the traditional authoritarian family structure, in which power is still in the hands of the elders, especially the men. Since the proportion of older people in India still remains low, old age has not become the commonplace it has in the Western world. This will change within the next generation: soon India will, in absolute terms, have the largest number of people over seventy worldwide. Exactly what effect this will have on traditional authority and the wisdom associated with old age remains to be seen.

It is significant that I met no one over the age of sixty. This is now the average life expectancy in India. At the time of Independence it was only thirty-eight – about the same as that of industrial Manchester in the 1830s.

2.   Marital status

Married: 29
Single: 42
Widowed: 2
Unknown: 2

About 40 per cent of the men I met were married. This is, to some degree, a reflection of the relative youth of the sample. I was struck by the number who said they were due to marry 'soon' or 'next year'. Indeed eight said this, almost 20 per cent of those not yet married. Only three said they had no intention of marrying. These were all middle-class and well off, and they identified strongly as gay men. Such people are less constrained by the perception of marriage as a contract between two families that provides the only guarantee of social security against sickness, unemployment, old age and loss, which is how it is perceived by poorer people. Indeed, marriage is seen as an inescapable social duty, even by many men whose preference is for their own sex. A few saw this as a burden, but the majority looked forward to it with a remarkable absence of anxiety. Having children is associated not only with security, but equally with a powerful sense of cultural continuity. Many found it incomprehensible that I had no children. 'Who will perform the last rites for you?' one man asked.

3. Place of origin

Delhi: 16
Uttar Pradesh: 20; of whom
       Lucknow: 6
       Gorakhpur: 3
       Uttarakhand: 3
       Kanpur: 2
       Aligarh: 2
       Meerut: 1
       Ghaziabad: 1
Haryana: 5
Punjab: 1
Rajasthan: 3
Jammu and Kashmir: 1
Bihar: 7
Orissa: 1
West Bengal: 5
Meghalaya: 1
Sikkim: 1
Assam: 1
Nagaland: 1
Maharashtra: 1
Madhya Pradesh: 4
Andhra Pradesh: 0
Tamil Nadu: 4
Karnataka: 1
Kerala: 1
Wouldn't say: 1

Some of the reported places of origin are misleading. People often refer to their family's native place as their home, even when they themselves were born in Delhi; this is especially true when they are keen to maintain their language and sense of cultural belonging. One man insisted he is from Tamil Nadu, although he was born and lived all his life in Delhi.

It was surprising how few men actually described themselves as natives of Delhi – less than one-quarter. This suggests that migrants are over-represented in the men who come to the Park, which, in turn, may be a consequence of the fact that they are separated from their families. On the other hand, it may be a fair reflection of the extent of migration into Delhi over the past thirty years. Certainly, this would be in keeping with the approximately fourfold increase in population during that time.

4. Occupation

Industrial worker:	7
Service sector (hotels, etc.):	8
Government service:	5
Armed forces:	6
Police:	2
Security guard:	1
Marketing:	4
Shopworker:	2
Finance:	5
Management:	4
Academic/teaching:	4
Self-employed:	6
Student:	5
Office worker:	2
Unemployed:	6
Mechanic:	2

Rickshaw driver:	1
Sex worker:	5
Beggar:	1

There is an extraordinary range of occupations, from the most privileged to the most wretched. In this sense, amongst the men who have sex with men, there really is a levelling element, a freemasonry of desire and need which transcends the usual social categories. (Although there were exceptions. Some said they couldn't possibly enter into a relationship with someone who was not from the same background or was of a different religion; but these were few.)

However, there is still a disproportionate number of the more self-confident classes – business people, those with a higher professional status. People from these groups tend to be far more comfortable than those who work in factories or fields with the idea not so much of 'being gay', but of seeking out other men for 'homosex'. This distinction – between identifying as gay and expressing a liking for same-sex relationships – is very significant. It is at the heart of the difference between a gay identity (a concept that mystifies the great majority) and male-to-male sexual activity.

The location of the Park helps determine the composition of its clientele: for example, because the Park is not far from several five-star hotels, the number of hotel workers is considerable. Many men who are drawn to same-sex relationships work in this sector. There is a distinct impression among these employees that tourists, foreigners, Westerners are likely to be more tolerant and open in their sexual attitudes; some entertain the hope that one of them may take up with a young Indian and whisk him away to Germany or America. In this way, a combination of sensibility and ambition impels young men who are aware of their attraction to men to seek work in this part of the service sector.

The cantonment area is not far from the Park; with members of the armed forces – army, air force, border security force and central

13

police reserve force – all stationed in camps nearby, it is hardly surprising that a large proportion of those who frequent the Park work for some kind of military organisation. Similarly, since Delhi is the seat of government, and the government is a major employer, there is also a number of government servants. This category covers a large variety of occupations, from secretaries in the ministry to peons and messengers.

The very broadness of these categories introduces an important consideration: a tendency for interviewees to claim for their work a status it does not necessarily have. For example, all of those who own their own businesses should not necessarily be thought of as among the most affluent: the business itself might be something as modest as a vegetable stall or a small clothing shop in Chandni Chowk. Likewise, those who say they are 'private service' may be either in the employment of a transnational company or they may be working as a domestic servant for a rich family. I met one man who had come from Meerut for an interview for the post of 'human resource development officer' in a brewery. He himself recognised that this was only a euphemism for a hirer of labour.

Another complication results from the element for self-definition involved in the interview process, a factor that becomes most noticeable in an examination of the sex industry. Those who acknowledge themselves to be sex workers are not the only ones who take advantage of the fact that money can be made in the Park. Some of the unemployed, students and those in very low paid jobs make a bit extra as opportunistic, casual workers in the sex market. So although they do not list this as their main employment, they do exploit their opportunities for making anything that might be offered for their services.

Some men travel a long way for their outings in the Park. There is always a sprinkling of people from Old Delhi or Transyamuna; but the majority are from west and south Delhi, which, although they contain pockets of poverty, are middle-class residential areas. If the Park had been close to Chandni Chowk, for instance, the profile of the people would have been very different; but in that part of Delhi there is no comparable place which offers the leisure and space necessary for my more or less informal research.

Another way of trying to understand what appeared to be the higher status than a representative sample of Delhi would have produced is to examine in which language the discussions were held. Those who could speak English fluently did so, since their English was better than my Hindi. Those who had to speak Hindi, on the whole, belong to the less educated and therefore the poorer strata. It worked out like this:

Hindi: 41
English: 32
Mixture: 5

It is clear that there are far more English speakers here than in Delhi as a whole. However, appearances are, as always, deceptive. Those who are not from the Hindi belt of India tended to speak English with me, even if not very well: men from Tamil Nadu and from the northeast chose not to speak Hindi. Indeed, one or two of them were less familiar with it than I was, even though some of them had lived in the city for many years. On the other hand, a number of people were keen to practise their English, even if it was not very good.

Once again, there is a clear bias to the middle class as compared with the population of India as a whole. This does not so much indicate that the people of Delhi are more well-to-do than the rest of India (although they are), as that the group which comes to the Park is more socially secure and well-educated than the people of the city as a whole.

This is not necessarily a disadvantage when it comes to making a judgement on whether or not the consciousness of being gay, of identifying as a gay man, is a feature of the better-off men in Delhi. Indeed, it made the division even more clear between those who identify as gay and those who – generally the poorer and less educated – simply have sex with men without classifying or categorising it in a way that would be familiar to a Western observer. Both groups were sufficiently well represented to make it possible to come to some tentative conclusions, as will appear.

II

First of all, I looked at the testimonies of those who are married. One question I asked each of them was whether his wife knew anything about his sexual attraction to men and about his sexual activity with them. Although only one man replied in the affirmative, there was some subtlety in how they defined the word *know*. Denial that she could possibly know anything was often mitigated. Many agreed that there is a knowing of the heart. That, they explained, means an awareness on the part of the wife of some affective absence, an intuitive sense that there is something wrong with or missing from the conjugal relationship. On the other hand, some were adamant not only that their wives could neither know nor even suspect, but that they were not even aware that such things existed.

'My wife knows nothing':	17
'She may feel something is wrong':	7
'She is unhappy with our sex life, but doesn't know why':	3
'She knows but cannot accept':	0
'She knows and accepts':	1

A considerable majority claimed that their wives knew nothing about their liking for men. Of course, this may well represent the confidence of the male whose cultural prerogative is to set limits, even to what his wife may be permitted to know. On another level, it may also indicate a desire to protect himself from any acknowledgement that his wife might indeed know, for this would cause him great pain and shame. However that may be, certain duties and obligations are assigned to the roles of husband and wife, and it is not uncommon for people to act out these roles without their feelings being engaged as they would be in Western culture. Thus, a good wife or a good husband is one who behaves according to a set of rules, who adheres to a revealed, known and agreed code of conduct. To refer to a 'good marriage' is thus not necessarily to comment on the quality of a relationship.

Many men made the point that women do not know what to expect when they marry, that they cannot, for instance, know what is a 'normal' pattern of intercourse; and if the husband is either less than enthusiastic or overexacting, the wife will adapt herself to that, without questioning too insistently the demands her husband makes on her (or, in this case, fails to make). Of course, this underestimates women's capacity for listening to their own bodies, as well as the consolation and knowledge they gain through talking to each other and sharing their experiences.

Yet the elevation of women (by men) in Indian society has a far darker side; namely, it also covers the conviction that they are, in other ways, lesser beings. Contempt is the obverse of an exaggerated homage paid officially to women or, more usually, to Woman. The abstraction becomes the focus of their reverence, sometimes to the cost of real flesh and blood. The Family is often the object of similar deference, despite the harm that is sometimes committed within its sacred precinct against women and children.

By no means all of these married men made their predilection for men appear unproblematic. Some were assailed by strong feelings of shame (rather than guilt), although some felt keenly that they were betraying their wives. They insisted that they could not help it. In this they were gratefully accepting one of the excuses and alibis held out to men, and sometimes supported by women themselves, that the sexual needs of men are more urgent and imperious than those of women, and will not be repressed. Even this, in traditional Indian culture, rebounds upon women, for, according to the Shastras, women are eight times more sexually charged than men. Thus, it is the woman's intense desire that governs sexual relations, a behavioural model that is echoed throughout the world.

I had some of the most poignant conversations with that minority who admitted they thought their wives must be aware that something is wrong. These men generally said they love their wives, and they revealed a tenderness for them that was not expressed by all of the married interviewees. This is not necessarily a criticism of cultural norms that differ from those in the West; but in a culture that is, however slowly, in the process of transformation, those norms are shifting, and such treatment of women is coming to be seen more and more as unjust and unacceptable. [It is very difficult not to be, on the one hand, either too dismissive of or too deferential towards traditional cultures; and on the other, either too enthusiastic about the Western tendency to universalise its own experience or too disparaging of the self-congratulation and complacency of the West in its understanding of interpersonal relationships.]

Some men clearly felt great distress, either at their irreconcilable sexual needs or at the lack of openness in their relationships with their wives. One man in particular came close to tears when he spoke about his wife and her unsuspecting (and, he thought, misplaced) confidence in him. Shailendra, twenty-eight, asked: 'Do you think I should see a psychiatrist? I thought marriage would put an end to these shameful desires. . . . I try to overcome this feeling of being attracted to men, and I pray it will go away. Sometimes, for a month or two, I think I have conquered it, but it always comes back, stronger, it seems, than before.'

Another, older man in his fifties, who would identify himself only as H. N., admitted that he is secretive and ashamed of his sexual needs. 'I feel badly whenever I come here. It is a sin, and that is how I was brought up to regard it. It is against our religion, which regards it as a crime against nature. I feel badly towards my children as well as towards my wife. God knows why this happens. But I cannot stop it. It has upset my life, turned it upside down.'

Both these men avoided giving their names: Shailendra introduced himself as 'Naveen', shedding his alias only when he judged that it was safe to do so. This was symptomatic of a wider tendency to attribute responsibility for sexual needs they could not reconcile with their view of the world to another identity, another place, another person: someone else (even if that someone was myself) made me do it; Delhi caused it to happen; it was a dream; it happened when I was sleeping (sleep and dreams are recurring metaphors); it occurred when I was under the influence of alcohol, in an altered state of consciousness.

There are two common and interlinked elements in the subgroup of men who are more sensitive to the feelings of their wives. One is the conviction that the wife knows or feels intuitively some emotional absence in him ('a desertion of the heart', one man said); the other is a strong sense of the injury he has inflicted upon her. Pradeep, still only twenty-five and from Jhansi, was married at eighteen. His bride was only fifteen. I asked him if his wife had any idea of his liking for men. He replied: 'She knows and she does not know. Many women, somewhere in their heart, sense something missing. Their husband's attentions have wandered elsewhere. They may be unhappy, knowing that something is not as it should be, but they may not be able to say what it is. This makes it more likely that she will blame herself, because for many women, their husband remains a god. And gods do not err. Women feel things in their heart, in their fingers, in their spirit. They have an understanding which does not need words. *Kya karega?*'

This struck me as one of the most truthful insights, because it is so painful. Pradeep feels keenly for his wife and is wounded by his inability to broach the subject of his sexual preference openly. He lives very uncomfortably with this knowledge and his apprehension of his wife's sentiments, but he can neither give her reassurance nor stop himself from coming to the Park.

19

One twenty-four-year-old, married for nine months, finds it impossible to conceal from his wife that something is wrong. He is impotent with her: 'I do not desire her, and my *lund* will not become hard. I am very sad. I have been to many sex doctors and quacks in Old Delhi. I have taken medicines, Ayurvedic and herbal, I have drunk tonics and remedies to strengthen my blood. I changed my diet, I remained abstinent for four weeks, but nothing changed. My wife is very patient and loving, but that only adds to my discomfort and humiliation. The only thing that gives me an erection is being with a man. I feel bad, because I am not worthy of her affection and patience. But I cannot say to her why I am unable to make love to her.'

Rawat, a thirty-year-old man who works in a bank, believes his wife suspects that he has another woman in Delhi, because he does not go home as often as he should. 'This thing [that is, having sex with men, a euphemism that was to become familiar, as was the question, "Are you in this line?", which made it sound like a profession] comes into a marriage, and it spoils everything between a husband and wife. But once you have discovered this, you cannot go back. My wife is angry sometimes, her mood becomes dark if I do not want sex. I do not feel affection for her, so I do not even like to touch her. She becomes wild and then she weeps. I cannot tell her the fault is not hers, but mine. She thinks she is to blame. She says "Am I ugly that you do not want me?" She thinks her legs are too hairy, her body too fat. I do not find her attractive. Quite the opposite in fact. But I feel bad, so naturally I do not want to be at home, and I go there infrequently.

'But we have done our duty. We have three children. I give her money. She has security. But you cannot feign desire or affection. You cannot create it when it is not there. You cannot pretend that you want someone who repels you.'

It is difficult to know whether the men who feel the pain of their estrangement from their wives are closer to the common experience than those who affirm there is no problem, and who are content to abuse their already considerable male privilege by doing whatever they want and keeping it from their wives, just as they keep from them so many other things – how much money they spend on themselves, whether they drink, where they go with their male friends, the details of their work. After all, women must accommodate themselves to only receiving such knowledge of their husbands' lives as they deign to grant them.

One channel of unwilling communication is opened when the wife contracts a sexually transmitted disease from her husband, the danger of HIV infection imparting a new gravity to this unconscious exchange of information. No one in India knows how far HIV is spread by men who have sex with men. Official statistics show that 'homosexual contact' is a negligible conduit of infection; but that is because very few men will talk openly about it.

This danger provides the impulse for the outreach work in the Park conducted by NAZ. This is a sexual health project, of which male-to-male sex is a major component. NAZ promotes safe sex and a wider understanding of the means of transmission of HIV. There is a growing number of women and their newly born children infected with HIV, transmitted by the sexual activity of men, of which they, for the most part, know nothing. This, already a trauma for many individuals, is yet another social disaster waiting to overtake the complacency and denial of the authorities. Only the extent of this problem is not yet clear; that it will occur is a certainty.

Nalin, now thirty-three, has been in the army for thirteen years. Two years ago, he was infected with gonorrhoea as a result of unprotected sex with one of the *khotis* in the Park (that is, the passive participants, whose 'feminised' behaviour distinguishes them from the supremely, sometimes aggressively, macho *giriyas*, as the *khotis* call their partners). The sexual contact occurred on the day before he went home on leave to Rajasthan. The same night he had sex with his wife and passed the infection on to her. 'She was very upset. Of course, I could not tell her the truth. She could not imagine how this came to her. I made the mistake of blaming her. Even though she had certainly had no relationship with anyone but me, she seemed to accept that it was her own fault. She thought maybe she had not kept herself clean enough. But she was so hurt by this, I could not bear to see her suffer. I told her I had been with a prostitute in GB Road in Delhi. I said to her, "Life in the army is very tough, and men sometimes get lonely. That was why I had sought release in this way." I said I was sorry and begged her to forgive me. She did. She had to, because she had no real choice.

'Afterwards, I noticed that there was a change in her attitude towards me. Not on the surface, which continued as if nothing had happened. It was altogether at a deeper level. My parents, too, were cool. I felt that I had spoiled my family life. I said to myself that I would never do this again. But I did. And I do. The only difference now, I always make sure I carry a condom in my pocket.

'But once the relationship of trust is broken, it cannot be mended. My wife does not enjoy sexual relations with me now. She will do, but her body is tense, clenched, as though she wants to draw away from me. We have a child, a little boy who is nearly three years old. But I know that her body and her mind are both closed against me now. I cannot help it, and I cannot do what is necessary to restore things. I cannot give up my desires. Going home is now always a problem for me. The innocence of my wife is destroyed and so is her faith in me. That is the worst thing.'

Those men who were convinced that their wives remained in complete ignorance of their sexual activities outside the home had for the most part come to terms with the need for secrecy. They said, 'What would be the point of telling her?', depending upon the culturally accepted powerlessness of women, certain that such information would only make their wives unhappy. H. N., for example, said: 'Of course my wife cannot know. What would she do if I told her? There could not be a divorce, because such things are rare in India. All that would happen is that she might tell her relatives, and they would humiliate me in order to stop this behaviour. They would make my life very difficult. Divorce would take everything through the courts. It would become known, and bring shame to her family, my family and the children. That would not be allowed to happen.'

Some of the men who said they were due to be married shortly have already made arrangements for the future concealment of their sexual preferences. Nataranjan, twenty-eight, from Orissa, who insists he is not a gay man, has nevertheless worked out a strategy that will permit him to continue the life he presently enjoys: 'When it comes to marriage, it is our Oriya custom that the *buha*, or bride, should come to know everything about the husband's household before marriage. She must learn what food her prospective father-in-law likes, she has to become familiar with the routine of the house, she must discover the personality of the mother-in-law, so that misunderstandings may be avoided. There are supposed to be no secrets, so that she can adapt to whatever she may find there. This is a problem for me. My work is here in Delhi, and I cannot return there to live.

'There are things in my life my wife cannot know. The best thing will be if she stays with my parents in Bhubaneshwar and I remain here, going home maybe twice a year. Many marriages in India are like this. Men must travel far away for the sake of their work. The women sometimes accompany them, sometimes not. With separation, there is less chance that people will fight or quarrel, because they do not come to know each other so intimately. Men who want to have sex with men can do this when they are living apart from their wives. But if you stay in the same house, the family will also ask so many questions – why are you late? who have you been with? what have you been doing? It is their right to do so; there is no secrecy in families, so this is why I shall wish to keep a part of my life separate from them.'

Jaspal, twenty, will also marry next year. Marriage holds no terrors for him. 'I like both men and women, although I've never had any experience with a woman. We will have two children, a boy and a girl. I will not stop having sex with men, why should I? It isn't a question of right and wrong, it is the way we are. Men are like this. What can there be wrong with enjoyment? I will not tell my wife, no. No problem.'

Arun, thirty, explains the changes he has made in his life since he married. He has now been married for three years, and he and his wife have a twelve-month-old daughter. Arun has a small shop selling children's clothes near Jor Bagh. He has the comfortable appearance of a contented married man, the growing corpulence that comes from regular and copious meals. He says that he was 'always for homosex' before he was married. 'But I do it less now. Sometimes I come to the Park, but mostly I have sex with friends I can call up when I feel like it. I am happy with my life. I have a good business, and we have bought an apartment, one floor of a new house in Safdarjung enclave. We can't afford a whole house. We do not stay in the joint family, but my parents are not far away.

'Now that I'm married, I have to be careful. I do not wish to hurt my wife. I do not want to cause any distress to my family. I am married only for social reasons, but in India those reasons are very compelling. I prefer men, I am quite sure of that, but in our country, no one can remain unmarried. Since my marriage, I control my desires for men, and I come here only occasionally – once a month maybe.

'It is very difficult to control one's desires and to redirect your sexual energy towards women as an act of will. But duty, you know, is a very powerful part of our life; and you do it because you know you have no alternative. I think of men's bodies when I have sexual relations with my wife, that is how I deal with it. My wife knows nothing. I cannot tell her. If I did so, what would she do? She can go nowhere and neither can I. I respect her and I love her. Love is not like your idea of love in the West. Love grows through being together; it is more like a deepening friendship. You know you are to be companions for life. We are a partnership. I have a good business: clothing is like food, it will always be needed. I sometimes wish it could be different, that I could be open about my life. But you have to live where you are, and within the limits that are set for you by family, by society, by custom, by your own needs.'

Kuldeep, thirty, married with one child and living in south Delhi, works in the Ministry of Environment. He is very concerned that his liking for men should not interfere with his married life. He always carries a condom. He likes men and women equally. With men he both *karta hai aur karvata hai*, that is, he is active and passive.

'I have no problem with an arranged marriage. Arranged marriages are not conspicuously less successful than your love-marriages in the West. An arranged marriage is a structure, a carefully built edifice, in which two families must make their home. The arrangements made by loving parents are the cement which binds the families together. Women do not know what to expect when they marry, but neither do men for that matter. But the context of marriage, deeply embedded in the social fabric, anchors it, in a way that love, what may be a passing inclination, can never do.

'I do not like to deceive my wife. I keep it to a minimum, maybe twice a month. There is always the question of place – no one in Delhi has anywhere to go, so sometimes your escapades are limited by factors over which you have no control. Then you have to make sure that people are clean and honest. Sometimes, I wait until my wife and our child have gone to her home, and then I can invite people to the house. But you have to be careful. I know of men who have been blackmailed by others they have met, and they have had to pay a lot of money to keep them quiet.

'I think about men for much of the time, but I do not do very much. I feel it is – or ought to be – forbidden. But I also care for my wife very much. She is good to me, and I will do nothing to damage that. The thing is, I cannot help myself. I would control it if I could. Sometimes I wish I had never found out about this thing, then I would be carefree. I would then be like her; I could live for her, as I believe she lives for me. I might have been happy if I had not known. But this is my fate, I do know, and I have to live with it. I've known since adolescence that I am different from other men.'

Most of the married men have a high regard for their wives; and although this doesn't prevent them from having sexual relationships with men, they show considerable respect not only for marriage itself, but for the wives whom family, fate or misfortune have destined for them.

Rashid is a garment worker in Okhla. He had sex with other boys as an adolescent and, although he has been married for fifteen years, has never stopped doing so. Recently, Rashid's wife came to Delhi; she went into a nursing home because although they have been married for 15 years, they have not yet had children. They had tried all kinds of medicines, had been to doctors and specialists in Gorakhpur, and had both taken traditional herbal recipes for barrenness, but to no effect.

'She was having very irregular periods – every two weeks, then six weeks, then weekly. We went to a gynaecologist in Delhi, and he recommended she come into hospital for two weeks. That cost one thousand six hundred rupees, so it was a good thing that I had been able to save out of my earnings. Now she is pregnant. The baby is due in February [in three months' time]. We are very happy. The pregnancy has been normal, although naturally we are always anxious about her. The family is overjoyed.

'My family said to me "If no child comes, divorce her." But I would never do that. I am just happy that I have worked so hard and was able to pay for the treatment without taking a loan. I love my wife, and I like sex with her. But real pleasure for me comes from sex with a man who is also a friend. I do not like a man to come and do like that behind a tree and then run away as if he has snatched a chain or a purse.'

The cultural pressure to conform and to marry affects even the few men who insist they will not do so. Rohan, thirty, a gay-identified man, will not marry, even though he admits: 'Sometimes I long to be married, simply for the companionship. I would love the security that comes with going home each day. How comforting it must be! How sweet it is to have someone waiting for you. I have one friend who is gay. He is in a joyless marriage which he entered because of convention. He does not like to have sex with her, nor even to touch her. She naturally becomes moody, sulky, because she cannot understand why he treats her so. She thinks it is cruelty, which in a way it is. I respect women too much to marry without telling my wife about my sexual needs. And a woman who could accept that, not simply accept it because I am a man and therefore powerful, and she is a woman and without power; but accept that this is the nature of our sexuality, that she understands it, just as I would understand her, if she had similar needs. But I think that is impossible.'

Quite rare, no doubt. But not impossible. I met one man, a social activist who is married to a journalist. They met independently of their families and became friends long before marriage was suggested. Nila accepts her husband's attraction to men; and she herself has had extra-marital relationships: 'This only strengthens our friendship. We are committed to one another. For our families, we are the ideal couple. We are both successful in our way. We are inseparable friends; and friendship is a good basis for honesty, mutual respect and acceptance of each other. We never get emotionally involved with the people we meet outside our marriage. That is the way to make it last. We never use outsiders to threaten each other with. We have been married for five years, and I never worry about where he is, any more than he worries about me, because we both know the other will come home at the end of the day. My parents are becoming agitated because I'm nearly thirty and we don't have children. That is the next thing. But I cannot see any reason why we should not manage this as we have managed everything else. I spent three years at university in the USA, and my husband has family in Vancouver. Yes, we have been exposed to Western ideas and values, if that is how you want to describe it. But I think the interplay of East and West is more subtle than that makes it sound; we have absorbed certain values from our own culture and others from our education and experience. These can exist together quite comfortably.

'It may be regarded as hypocritical, to be living a conventional family life here, but no one is harmed by it. If the system forces us to live in ways that make us not entirely true to ourselves, then we should use those conventions and modify them to make a decent life. Of course this is a privilege. Most gay men or bisexual men do not have anything like our advantages. That is unfortunate, and I'm sorry for them. But it certainly isn't a reason for us to sacrifice the advantages we have.'

Ram Singh, thirty-three, married only four years ago in his native Rajasthan, much against his will and only when family pressures became irresistible. 'If a woman in Rajasthan is married and has no children, she will be shunned. For the first three years after marriage, we remained childless. The women in the village would go to my wife and say, "What is wrong?" Then they would say to her and her family, "Please do not let this woman go out in the early morning"; because if they saw her on their way to work or to a business appointment or even to labour in the fields, they would cancel whatever they were going to do, because to see a childless woman in the early morning was an omen of ill luck. Such things happen all the time.

'Relationships between men and women can be very limiting. Maybe the discussions we hear about other forms of sex are making some older men realise that the life they have lived is very restricted. They now want to try new things. Some discover they want homosex.

'In the past, a man would accept that this was his life. A wife is for sex, *bas*. You just put it in, ten minutes later it is finished. You then sleep in your own bed, somewhere else. She provides food when you want it, sex when you want it, but she feels it is not a matter of great interest to her. In families, sex often stops as soon as the children grow old enough to know what is going on. In the village, everyone sleeps close together, there is no privacy.

'We have one child. I do not want more. I've had a vasectomy, so we shall not. My wife, I see her perhaps two or three months in the year. It is enough, for her as well as for me.'

III

Even the men who declared that their wife's ignorance of their activities caused them no problem were not as insensitive as this may sound. Indeed, some even affirmed that good sexual relations with their wives were enhanced by their sexual contact with men. Gautam, an electrician, a cheerful exuberant man in his forties, has six children between the ages of four and fourteen. Brimming over with energy and joy, he makes no attempt to justify his enthusiasm for sex. He says that he has sex with his wife almost every day and that she enjoys it as much as he does. He expresses surprise when I ask him if he feels guilty towards her: 'Why should I? Wives are there to look after their husbands, just as husbands are there to look after their wives.'

It is clear that this is not a reciprocal looking after: there is an implicit division of labour here – the man provides for the family and the wife services him. In any case, as I was to learn, in South Asia, *guilt* is not the appropriate term to describe the emotions that are prompted by extramarital relationships: *shame* is a more accurate word. Guilt is personal, introspective; shame is fear of public disclosure, loss of face and status.

Gautam, speaking from within the remorseless logic of this unequal relationship, says, 'If there is something missing in the marriage, the husband must go outside. This can happen only in Delhi.'

He also provided some insight into what makes a happy marriage – for a man. 'Looking after the children, that is her work. When I come home, I have only to say "Chup" and the children will be quiet and get out of my way. She cooks the meals, which she does very well. Very fine. I give her fifteen hundred a month.' 'How much,' I ask, 'does it cost to feed a family of eight for one month?' 'You must ask my wife that. Every day she produces rice, vegetables, roti and dal. If there is no money, the dal is watered down. We are never hungry. We live in a two-room set near the airport, which costs eight hundred rupees a month. We have a few *bighas* of land near Gorakhpur, and sometimes relatives bring some rice or wheat. They receive some money from the milk from the four buffaloes. My wife does no paid work – with six children, that would not be possible.' I come back to the question 'How can she feed you all on fifty rupees a day?' Gautam insists that he does not know. He only earns the money; it is her job to do what she can with it: 'You must ask her.' He says, 'Do I look ill-nourished? Do I look as if I am starving?'

Amit, a mechanic with the army, goes home less often than he should. He says: 'My wife is a simple woman. She has no idea that such things exist. She cannot know. It has never come to her experi-ence. She will not suspect. She knows that men like the company of other men. This is very common in India – friendship between men is very important. There is no question in her mind that it could involve anything else.'

Ibrahim, manager of a hotel in Karol Bagh, believes that what he does with men does not hurt his wife. He says: 'I love her, and I do not love the men I meet, although friendship may be there. I would do nothing to hurt her. We have a good sexual relationship, we enjoy two or three times a week. But there is something else that I need. It does not affect her.'

Prasad, thirty-three, owner of a garment factory, says he is happy in his marriage: 'When we first married, nine years ago, my wife and I would have sex three times a week, but since the children were born, this happens less frequently, sometimes on a Saturday or Sunday . . . After so many years of marriage, sex must become less important. Many men I know say that interest in sex is almost finished when the last child is born. I have one friend who tells that his wife does not expect any further contact after their third child. She thinks that sex for its own sake is unnatural. She was shocked that he would even consider such a thing.'

Ram Singh, who has been in the Indian air force for fifteen years, married four years ago, when he could no longer resist family pressure to get married. 'I love her, but it is not real love. I would rather have a relationship with a man, although I enjoy sex with my wife.'

Sabhu leads a life of reckless promiscuity with both men and women, and is more dismissive of his wife than any of the other men I met. He roams the city at night, going into public toilets, sometimes visiting female sex workers. He reminded me strongly of working-class men in Victorian England: their wives stayed home, looked after the children and serviced their husbands when required. Sabhu and his wife have three children, all boys, under the age of five. He says: 'She stays at home. Sometimes she goes to see her relations. If I go home, there is food prepared; if I don't, I will eat it tomorrow. She does not ask me where I go. It is not her business. It is a man's job to go and earn the money, and hers to use it to look after the family. His place is outside and hers is at home. I do not like to spend much time at home. It is noisy and crowded. When I want to have sex with her, she will do, because that is also her work. She knows nothing of my life outside and never will. I have one girlfriend, and I am going away with her to Rishikesh for three days. My wife knows only that I am going on a pilgrimage. It has nothing to do with her.'

One gay-identified man, well aware of these troubling complexities, insisted that he does not get involved with married men: 'For the most part, they are deceiving their wives, and more often than not deceiving themselves too. If a man is married, he will pretend that he has sex with men only for discharge, only because he is separated from her, or because she will not do all the things he wants. He will never commit himself to another man; and that kind of sex I certainly do not need or want.'

This was, however, an isolated example. The nature of most sexual encounters rarely gives much scope for discussion of the marital status of the partner.

Women are used as scapegoats in many of the apparently plausible reasons which men advance to justify their relationships with men. One of the most common was Indian women's alleged lack of erotic imagination and repugnance for a variety of sexual behaviours. This was mentioned by ten of the married men, that is, 34.8 per cent. The formulation was in each case remarkably similar. In the men's own words:

'An Indian wife will never suck. She does not even know of such things, but permits only straight fucking. I could not ask her to do anything else. She would think I was mad or depraved.'

Tushar, twenty-eight, housekeeper in a five-star hotel

'Women understand nothing beyond basic sexual behaviour, that is, straightforward sexual intercourse. Men need variety and change. This a woman can never understand, because she wants her husband only. She depends on him. She doesn't want anything else.'

Pradeep, thirty-eight, member of the Central Reserve Police Force

'I am happy with my wife, but I like also to do things that only men do. My wife will accept only frontal intercourse. If I try to turn her over, she will think I am being cruel. She does not really like sex. After our baby was born, she is no longer interested in making love. It makes life very frustrating. I come here to find what I need. If I cannot find this at home, why will I stay there?

'I do not say that it is fair for women; in every way life is against them. But that is not a reason for me to deny myself. There is more opportunity for men to find what they want; not a lot more opportunity, but some. And there is no reason to refuse that, just because women have no freedom at all.'

Ramesh, twenty-eight, debt collector and rose grower

'My wife enjoys sex as much as I do. But like most Indian women, she will perform only straight sex. I like to be sucked. I want this to be done by a woman, but for that you have to pay – maybe two hundred or three hundred rupees, I do not know. I have never done that. A friend told me of this place, where men will do it for enjoyment only. When I do here, I do not think it is a man, I close my eyes and it becomes a woman.'

Gautam, forty

'We have a good sexual relationship, we enjoy together twice a week or more. But there is something else I need. The only thing I do with men is suck. I do not like to enter or be entered. . . . I like to be sucked very much. . . . A woman cannot do it. You cannot expect women to understand some needs that men have. I came to know that I wanted this only after marriage. Before I married, I had no experience of sex at all. I was delighted with my wife; the marriage was arranged and I had no idea what to expect. She too likes sex. But even when we did three or four times in a week, I always felt some small dissatisfaction. I would go and do with my hand in the bathroom, even after just making love to my wife. I cannot help it.'

Ibrahim, twenty-eight

'They [women] will not do things. They will not suck. They will not allow a man to penetrate from behind. This means they do not want what men want. If I continue to desire, why should I be blamed? I am good to her. I do my duty. I give her enough money to bring up our children. I appreciate her. I show affection. I do not feel shame if I make friendships outside. Why should I? If I do something with the body of another man, this does not mean I am disloyal to my wife. I do not know why it is like this. This is the way men and women are made, what can I do?'

Prasad, thirty-three

'Women will allow only intercourse from the front. They will not take a husband's cock into their mouth. You can kiss her lips and even her breasts, but you may not place your mouth *niche*, down there. It will disturb and frighten her.'

Rashid

'I cannot play with her. It is for her a duty. Everything but straight intercourse in the dark is labelled No Entry.'

Man Singh, a man who has made a career in the army

The persistent story of women's 'refusal' struck me as a little too easy, too readily available. Bharat, in his mid forties, said, 'I like to be sucked. I do not ask my wife to do this, she will refuse.' I enquired, 'Have you ever asked her?' 'No, she would be insulted.' 'How do you know, if you have never asked her?' 'You do not understand,' he said coldly, turned abruptly and walked away.

Ram Singh, thirty-three, in the air force, spoke at some length about his wife. He maintains that sexual contact with a wife is limited. 'With an Indian wife, all that happens is penetration. You may kiss the lips and around the face, but there will be no tongue kissing. She will not suck your cock, and you may not kiss her genitals. If you should ever suggest such a thing, she will be very unhappy, because nobody ever does these things. She will think you are perverted. This is why ninety per cent of men who want sex with men want to be sucked. You cannot kiss her body, or maybe only her breasts, and you cannot even put your face near her private parts.'

The proportion of married men who spoke in this vein is too high to be ignored. It is significant that the conservatism of women's sexual behaviour is attributed to them by men: none of the husbands admitted to having asked their wives to vary the pattern of their sexual activities. Only one of them had tried something different – he confessed that he was drunk at the time – and was repulsed.

This suggests that the women – victims of marriage in every way – are further being called upon to bear responsibility for their husbands' drive to seek sexual satisfaction with men. Because they are not involved in these testimonies, their absence can be used as a kind of dumping ground for everything that the men do not wish to confront about themselves. Indeed, we may be close to the deeper reasons why most men cannot or will not admit to being gay (or its equivalent in Indian culture): the patient, submissive and immemorial silence of women.

This is not to deny such testimony. There is doubtless truth in what some of the men say. But it is truth based upon the partial, one-sided and non-negotiable relationship in which the wife is an unequal partner. The denial of her willingness to perform acts which the men desire is an oblique tribute to her: they believe she is above such things. Yet even that tribute is a denial of her humanity, because through it the men are trying to deny their own needs: by refusing to acknowledge that she could ever entertain such ideas, by seeking answers to their 'shameful' desires outside the primary relationship, they are also expressing their own shame. As long as women are expected to remain vessels of purity destined to bear the children (as well as the weight of their husbands' ideology) there can be no reciprocity in sexual relations. The men are also expressing their dissatisfaction in the nature of the sexual dynamic between men and women.

And some are certainly simply blaming women for their own sexual orientation. By saying 'she will not do what I need', they are offering a powerful justification for their presence in the Park. It is only a short step from this to saying 'she has driven me here'. It would be interesting to know what men who go to female sex workers say about their marital relationships. It may be that they would express a contempt for the female prostitutes similar to that which some of the men – especially those who penetrate – profess for the men they are impelled to meet in the Park.

One man, a security guard at a hotel, said: 'I like men, because men are tight. Women's bodies, after childbirth, become loose. I do not enjoy.'

There was certainly plenty of evidence to suggest that the *giriyas* in particular despise the *khotis* they use. This introduces another of the common justifications for men having sex with men: there are no women available; there is no way for a man to meet women casually in Delhi; it costs too much to go with women. With men it is easier, there are no consequences. Many even affirm that 'sex with men is safer' (which effectively blames women for STDs and HIV). Among some of those not yet married, men are said to be makeshift partners, who will be abandoned after marriage. Indeed, the earnest assurance that with marriage 'this thing will stop' of the younger unmarried men seems to turn readily into the complaint that 'she will not do all the things I want' of the older, married men. The only consistency between those who have not and those who have jumped the impermeable barrier of marriage is the blamelessness of men.

The unmarried men expressed it like this. Sandeep, twenty-seven: 'In our culture marriage is for life. It means one man and one woman.' When I asked him why he came to the Park for sex, he was severe: 'This is before marriage. I do this because I am not yet married. I would not do sex with a woman because I have too much respect for women. After marriage, I shall have no wish to do this any more. One man and one woman. And then, you grow up and your children learn how to treat their own future wives and husbands by your example. Then they will look after you when you are old. After marriage, that is when it is time to settle down. Until then, a man needs to have some outlet, some discharge for what is in his body.'

Abhijit, twenty-five, a hotel worker, was anxious to distance himself from his sexual activity. He says he likes sex *thora-bahut* [somewhat]. 'I am looking forward to the time when I will be married, so that I can leave all this and forget about it. I do not like sex with men, but there is no chance for me to meet women in Delhi.'

Vipin, twenty-six, said, 'When I come to be married, I will stop this habit. Marriage is a cure for it.' 'Is it a sickness then?' I asked. 'In a way, *yaar*, it's sick that young men cannot get women, so they do [it] together.' 'Have you ever been with a woman?' 'No, but when I do, I'm sure it will be what I want, what I'm looking for. I'm a normal young guy. I want all the things other young guys want – a car, nice house, travel, money, a good life.' 'Does wanting all those things mean that you want a wife as well?' 'Sure. Why not?' There was no doubt in his query. It was clear that he had consulted the index of normality among his peers and concluded that among the obligatory material symbols of success, a wife figured conspicuously. He was not listening to his inner needs.

Vinod, twenty-four, who has been married for nine months and has yet to consummate his marriage, sees it more tragically: 'I thought marriage would be the answer to everything, to all the confusion I had. That is why I married at twenty-three. All that happened was that I can no longer avoid my problem, which is that I am sexually drawn to men and not to women. My wife confided this to her brother, so now the whole family knows that I have been unable to do my duty. My father-in-law told me to see a doctor. But how can I tell the truth, even to a doctor? The shame this will bring would be worse than telling the truth. Only if I can make her pregnant, she might be satisfied. But first I think I must have some experience with a man, because then it may be easier to make love to my wife. I want to make a life with her, so that we can become a family like any other. Marriage has only shown me that the sort of arousal I thought it would bring I can achieve when I am with some of my men friends.'

A number of men indicated that they thought sex with men was a habit; and they meant a bad habit. Some hinted at its addictive quality and said that they knew it would be hard to break. Mahesh, a young man of twenty-three, said, 'Once you get into this line, you cannot break out of it. You are hooked for life. It is worse than Brown Sugar [a heroin derivative].' He seemed to me to be saying that he had discovered his liking for men but couldn't really tolerate the idea that it was an intrinsic need; so he likened it to an addiction, taking the responsibility away from the individual. This tendency to place responsibility elsewhere, as later emerged, was to be a common reaction.

Surinder, in the army for ten years, is not yet married. He says he does not like sex with men, but what choice is there? 'I will not go with women, because there is a risk of disease. It is safer with men. I like to fuck. I do not like men who like men, because I only want women. The young boys who behave like women, that is OK. I penetrate them. They get fucked. A man is someone who fucks. A woman is the one who takes it. So these boys who take it, they are like women. I will not make friends with them. I despise them. I do not like men who are not men, who pretend to be women. I sometimes give them twenty rupees. Some I like better than others. There is one boy [he indicates one of the *khotis*] if he is there, I will go with him, because he knows how to make me enjoy, and he enjoys also. But most of them just drop their pants and wait for you to enter them. They are timepass; they are only a substitute for the real thing.' Surinder has never had sex with a woman.

The rationalisation that they are only having sex with men pending marriage came up seven times among the unmarried men, a little over 16 per cent of the total. This was certainly the reaction of Subodh, twenty-seven, who frequently visits Connaught Place after his day's work, as ticket tout for a travel agency. He says: 'I am not yet married. I have to help my brother and sister finish their education. Until then, I cannot think of marriage. I am active. I am not gay. Gays are those who take from the backside. I met one man here two years ago, who asked me to do. I went to his place. I was very scared, but I enjoyed very much. I was surprised. Now I do. This is not my business, but sometimes, men give me five hundred rupees. I would like to have one good friend, but that is not easy in India. But this is not gay. After marriage, I will never come here.'

This was also the story of many married men whose work had brought them to Delhi. Migration is a powerful alibi for those separated from their families. It may also be true in some cases. Gurbaiv, who has been in the army for twelve years, says, 'My family is in Bengal. Here, I sometimes see blue films. I have sex with men. I do not like it. I am thinking of my wife only. I am interested in many things – sport, politics, books, as well as sex. I have sometimes been to the morning movie show in some Delhi theatres. Many men sit and do it *hath se* [with their hands].'

It is significant that many of the unmarried men projected the same feelings onto their parents that the married men attributed to their wives. Parents could not possibly be told. If they knew, they would throw me out, they would cut me off from the family. They would kill me (or it would kill them). To such assertions I sometimes said gently that there were very few instances in the world of parents killing their children on discovering their sexual orientation. Although I was well aware that such melodramatic declarations were really only a kind of metaphor, they clearly expressed the impossibility of broaching such subjects with their parents.

Jairam, twenty, was brought to the Park for the first time by the uncle with whom he lives in Delhi. This man is a policeman. 'I wanted to ask my uncle if he knew what goes on in this Park. I asked him what all the people were doing. I thought he must be knowing, since he is in the police, and they know what happens everywhere. I said nothing to him. I could not find the words. He is looking after me. He is elder to me. I wondered why he had brought me here. Perhaps he wanted to know if I am also like that.

'If my father and mother knew, they would be very shocked. We have a little land, but my parents have known nothing but the village. They will never have heard of such things. But I want to find out if my uncle knows or not. He has two children. He gives me two hundred and fifty rupees a week for pocket money. I do not know how to talk to him about these matters.'

Harish, a young man of twenty-one from Bhopal, is studying in Delhi to get a professional qualification in design. At the same time, he is working for a textile company which designs and manufactures garments for export. He earns Rs 4500 a month and is able to support himself as he studies. He lives in government accommodation for students who come from out of Delhi. Harish feels very lonely in Delhi.

'I got no support from my parents,' he complains. 'My father is a lecturer and my mother a teacher. It is not that they refuse me money or will not take care of my material needs. But my father is very aggressive, and he says the work I am doing is not a proper way to earn a living. He does not recognise the creativity in me. . . . My parents have conventional ideas about success. I cannot tell them about being gay. I can't say that I like it. If I had the choice of how to be in India, it would not be this. My parents have always been distant, I have never been able to discuss anything with them, even the smallest things, let alone something that affects everything in my life. It makes me feel I have been excluded from the family.'

Nishant, thirty-one, from a well-to-do family, is working in a chemicals factory in Delhi. He calls himself the failure in a family that expects success from its children. 'I cannot talk to my father. He is a very strong man, disciplined, controlling everything and everyone, including himself. He hates any sign of weakness. He thinks it is unmanly. I cannot show him that I am sitting alone in Delhi, crying.'

Vipin is working in his father's paint factory. It is a good job. He works hard and is well-paid, but is constantly under his father's eye. He comes to the Park on Sundays to enjoy. This, to him, represents escape: 'I cannot speak about sex to my father. It is forbidden. In India, a father is a father, not a friend.'

Sachin is nineteen, a student. Tomorrow, he is going to Varanasi, because it is the *varshi* ceremony for his grandmother, who died one year ago. He says: 'I do not believe, but I must go for the sake of the family. The conservatism of India compels me to do many things I do not want to do, and forbids me to do many other things I really want to do.

'My life is totally regulated by my parents. They do not like me to stay out late in Delhi because so many bad things happen – kidnappings, crimes of violence and so on. I'm allowed to stay out late if there is a disco or a party at college, but if I'm late, my father becomes very worried. I'm not allowed to roam in Delhi at night.

'There can be no honesty and openness between parents and children in India. When I used to ask my parents how a child comes to be born, they would never tell. When I asked them how I was made, they said, "We bought you in the bazaar at Kullu Manali." You half believe them and half don't. Whenever I would not drink my milk as a small child, my mother would say, "We'll have to take you back to Kullu Manali and exchange you for someone else who will drink his milk."

'I've had a smooth life. It makes me want everything. Until now I've been successful in everything I've done. But I know one day soon the conflict will come between what I want and what they expect of me. Love and authority are closely linked in family relationships in India. It is very hard to separate them, and most people never do.'

Premchand is twenty-three, living on the periphery of Delhi, where his family's ancestral land lies. He is a student, doing an export business course. His father is in the Ministry of Defence. 'If my parents knew, they would simply order me to stop this dirty habit. My father would not understand. Fathers do not talk to their sons. They tell them what to do. This does not include any discussion of what they tell them. The father may set an example or he may not. But whichever is the case, the son is expected to know right from wrong and to choose the right path.'

'If my father knew,' says Rajinder, twenty-two, 'he would kill me.' Surely, I said, that is a bit of an exaggeration. 'Well,' Rajinder amended, 'he would throw me out. You don't know them. He would think it disgusting and perverted. If an article comes in the newspaper about homosex, he and my mother are very loud in their condemnation of it. I don't know if they think something is wrong with me, and they want me to correct it. But you would have to hear them to believe how intolerant they can be.' I met Rajinder in Central Park. He is working in his father's embroidery factory in south Delhi, where nine people are employed.

Karim, a university lecturer in Lucknow, commented on the search by many young men in India for a substitute father, one they can confide in. 'I have found that many young men are looking for father-figures. For me, frankly, I find this a one-way process, neither rewarding nor interesting. Of course, a lot of older men are flattered by the attentions of a younger man, but I find they rarely have much to offer. I get bored by them. I cannot share ideas with them or talk about books I have enjoyed. A lot of young men seek out older companions because their own fathers are remote or authoritarian. They cannot bring to them any of the preoccupations of their youth. Unfortunately, I have little wish for them to bring such concerns to me either.'

It is not only parents who cannot know of men's sexual relationships with each other. Yusuf is eighteen. A tall, hungry-looking boy, friendly and open, he does not conceal his sexual orientation, at least when he is in the Park. He comes there almost every day, and he is very physical with his friends. He clowns and jokes freely, now dancing, now going through a pantomime of lovemaking, now pretending to be a pregnant woman. He is a professional, who has no other work than this.

He comes from Bihar and lives in one room with his brother and his brother's wife not far from New Delhi station. The wife is still only sixteen and, as yet, there are no children. The brother works in a factory which manufactures pumping machinery. Yusuf tells the family that he is working in a garment factory. He does not like the deception he must practise, but *kya karega*? Each morning, he leaves home around nine and returns twelve hours later.

Today, he is carrying a plastic bag of bananas for his lunch. He is very conspicuous in the Park and very successful. He is much in demand and can be seen disappearing into the jungle with one man after another. Some days he may earn two hundred rupees, others maybe only thirty or forty rupees. The most difficult times are in the rain and in winter, when Delhi is covered with a blanket of smoky fog and the temperature remains low. Even so, in the rain, he grins, it is sometimes easier to make money, because there are fewer people: those who do come are always more desperate to pick up someone and are therefore more likely to give handsome tips. Yusuf, although he left school at twelve, knows how to calculate to the last detail his chances in the highly specialised sex market in which he operates. Because he is living near Paharganj, where many Westerners stay, he is occasionally lucky enough to meet someone from the US or Germany. They are often generous to him. An American once bought him a lot of clothes, and gave him five hundred rupees. But he does not like operating too close to home. He insists on the necessity of absolute concealment from his brother, who is twenty-three and feels responsible for his younger brother. If he knew, says Yusuf, he would send me back home. Yusuf could imagine no more terrible fate.

It seems that the authoritarianism of families weighs heavily upon the unmarried men who have sex with men. Only after marriage does it work to their advantage; then they exploit the privileges which they earlier deplored, in order to practise a life of concealment and deception on their own wives and children. Occasionally, this breaks down, sometimes in the most unexpected ways, and the paternal mask of upright authority is shattered.

Girish is twenty-seven. Tall, fair-skinned and good-looking, with bronze-tinged hair, he had an English-language education in a private school, and works as a sales manager for an ice cream company. He identifies as gay. 'I had crushes on boys at school, which would come and go. One of these attachments was very strong and lasted for more than a year. I was sixteen at the time. We never talked about sex, but there was something between us which we did not put into words, let alone action. It created a kind of tension between us, but that was always very exciting. I always wanted to be with him. We were inseparable, linked by a bond which was never spoken of.

'One day I came out of school early. My friend was absent that day, and I felt bored. I came to our house where I expected to find no one but the servant. My mother had gone away with my young sister to her parents in Andhra. Instead, I found my friend, Mahesh, together with my father. They were both wearing only underpants.

'I could not believe what I saw. I went cold, and I remember I started to tremble violently. It was a double shock. My father! But the worst thing, which I worked out only later, was that the two people who were the most important to me in my life at that time both preferred to be with each other rather than with me. . . .

'He had always been distant from me, very strict. He supervised me very closely. I had no freedom. I believe now that he was looking for signs in me of something he knew was inside himself. I have no idea if this predisposition to liking men is genetic.

'When I was quite young, I used to have fantasies about my father. I used to dream of seeing him without any clothes, which of course never happened. I would dream of finding myself alone with him, my mother having vaguely disappeared in some way. I was too good a son to wish her dead, but I longed to be in a position where I alone was there to comfort him.

'After this incident, I could no longer take him seriously, and I pretended to despise him. It was a complete reversal of our relationship. He was afraid I would tell my mother, but of course I never would. Male solidarity, or at least a common liking for men, which I alone was aware of, prevented such treachery on my part, even though I felt he had betrayed me. Seeing him and my friend together like that crystallised something for me. What I had seen until then only as having a crush on boys became something else. It defined for me what I most wanted in life.

'My father tried to be friendly to me, but I couldn't return his overtures. I felt frozen inside. He made himself pathetic in my eyes. After being this remote godlike figure, he became despicable. I could not respect him. He owns a factory making steel utensils in east Delhi, about forty employees. I told him I had become a socialist and accused him of ill-treating his workers. This made him furious and he said, "Everything I've done I have done it for you." We have a nice house. I have never been deprived of anything I wanted. Materially, at least. I have one sister who is married and has three children.'

Only three men had actually told their families they are gay. Rohan is an articulate middle-class man of thirty. He is in marketing, with a qualification in business studies. 'I told my brother about it. There are just the two of us. After I had confided in him, he became somewhat distant from me. I noticed a perceptible cooling in our relationship. What made it worse was that he told our mother. She eventually came to accept it, although she too was cool at first. She is principal of a school. She is an intelligent woman. I was going to tell her, and it should have come from me, but he told her before I was ready to do so. He must have presented it to her in terms of Rohan has a problem, which was not the approach I was going to take. Fortunately, both have now come to an understanding, and I can be open with them and get support from them.'

Kamal owns a garment factory which employs between sixty and seventy workers. 'I came out to my family. They were not exactly rejecting, but I can't say they welcomed my disclosure. At first, they said it was a phase I would surely outgrow. I was already in my mid twenties by that time, so it was a very late phase, and I'd certainly finished all the growing I was going to do. They were tolerant, because they are educated people. They thought if they didn't object, it would pass, I would grow tired of it. I don't know what they expected. It has taken several years for them to recognise that it goes deeper than that. I don't discuss it with them now, but I believe they have become reconciled to it. I take friends home to them. I sometimes see my mother looking at my companion and thinking "Is he having a relationship with my son?" I know what she is thinking, although she is far too polite to say anything. It still bewilders them a little.'

Vijendra, thirty-five, is also from a well-off family. He is a lawyer; and when the question of his marriage kept coming up – 'which it did with increasing regularity when I was in my twenties' – he could stand it no longer and told his parents he could never marry because he preferred men. 'They were very shocked. I told them abruptly, because I could not bear that they should live in this mistaken perception of me. I said it was not a problem, but I would not marry. They said it was impossible and wanted to take me to doctors and psychiatrists. I told them it was not an illness. I liked it like this.

'Then they fell quiet. I thought they had accepted. For about six months nothing was said. Then they started to talk about marriage again, just as if we had never had the explosion in the first place. They had actually censored the knowledge out of their minds. I couldn't believe it. Now I live alone. I still see them regularly. They sometimes mention marriage. I will talk about anything else with them, but as soon as they start that I just walk out. I won't take part in any such discussion. But I don't think they can cope with the idea. So they have to pretend it was never spoken. The social conventions are stronger than reality. It has been a revealing episode.'

Nearly all the men who spoke about the awkward and painful relationships with their parents were middle class. It is significant that most of those who identified as gay were of a higher social status than those who made no mention of generational struggles with their parents. The only poor boy who spoke of having to conceal his sexual orientation was Yusuf, and he was hiding the fact that he is a sex worker from his brother. For most of the poorer men, the idea of being gay or of being homosexual scarcely arose. They sometimes said they liked homosex; but that is a far cry from assuming a gay identity or from perceiving homosexuality as a major determinant in their lives.

This question of consciousness is at the heart of this book.

Number of men who identify as gay:	14
Number of men who say they 'like to enjoy' with men:	12
Number of men who deny they like sex with men but do it 'for relief' or for money:	8
Number of men who say they like sex with men or used the word homosex:	30
Number of men who identify as bisexual:	1
Didn't say:	10

These categories, of course, overlap and need some explanation. They evolved only some time after my conversations with the men, because their accounts of their lives were often apparently contradictory; the distinctions and nuances appeared only after some reflection and, in many cases, after several meetings with them.

Less than one-quarter of the men identified as gay. They were almost exclusively middle-class, professional men, although one or two of the *khotis* also acknowledged the idea of being gay. But even the group which had been most open to Western influence and discourses around sexual politics, mainly English-speaking and educated to university level, did not see being gay as the main constituent of their identity. They did, however, express relief at being able to name this aspect of themselves. One man said, 'Yes, I am a gay [*sic*]. But I am also a Hindu, a Tamil, a Brahmin, a salesman, a son, a brother, a friend, a musician. Why would I give priority to one aspect of my identity over the others?'

Kamal, who is thirty-four, said: 'I spent my whole life looking for sex, until I found a gay social life. I was engaged on an obsessive search for purely sexual release until I met other gay men. I made friends with them, shared experiences and began to relax. Now I am very positive about being gay. Naming it offered me release from what had become an addiction to sex for its own sake. It gives me a secure base, a stability from which I can look for relationships. Once I had accepted that I was gay, it was almost like a conversion. I have a network of friends and social support. I can look outwards from this and not rush desperately into every sexual encounter, over-anxious to make a lasting relationship.

'Having said that, being gay does not engulf me. I am still many other things too. But being gay helps me to integrate all those parts of my life.'

Karim, who is in his fifties, is a historian at Lucknow University. 'Although I will stand up for being gay, I have never made either a virtue or a secret of it. All who know me are aware of my interests, but I have no wish to be an activist. Some of us, mainly academics and professional people, have set up a group with the objective of spreading truthful and factual information about homosexuality, disseminating awareness. We also plan to create an archive, with historical material about same-sex relationships. People should come to know that this is rooted in our Indian culture and is not – as some have tried to claim – yet another alien import from the West.'

Keshav is recognisably and assertively middle class. He is working as a representative of a pharmaceutical company. His father is a government official, and Keshav says he would prefer to work in government service, because there is security of employment there, and this is the most important thing to him. 'The private sector is too competitive, and I do not like to have my life dominated by work. I have so many more important things to do, including cultivating my relationships and pursuing my sex life. I do not want to be so tired after work each day that I am unable to go out and meet my friends.'

Keshav knew he was gay at the age of sixteen or seventeen. 'There was one boy in our school who was a real hero-figure. He was very handsome, attractive to girls, good at sport, very intelligent. He used to go around saying "I am gay, I am gay." That was in 1989, when being gay first started to be talked about in India. The fact that he announced this set a trend in the school. Many boys imitated him and went round announcing to the world that they too were gay. Some may even not have been; but since he was so charismatic and attractive, it was obviously the thing to be. It became fashionable. This made it all the easier for those of us who knew we were gay to speak out also. I knew I was like this, even though at school I never did anything about it, except say so to anybody who cared to listen. It was only when I got to college that I was prepared to go further.'

Rohan is an articulate man of thirty, working in an advertising agency. In college he had relationships with other boys, but they did not go very deep, constituting the typical adolescent fooling around. After finishing his education, he started to date girls. This he also enjoyed; it was only when he came to Delhi from his native Indore in Madhya Pradesh that his preference for men became clearer.

'Until then, my sexuality seemed to me amorphous, ambiguous. It was not clearly defined. Perhaps I was not ready to define it myself. It became more decisive only with maturity. Many young people are like this. It isn't until they have some defining experience that they become aware of what they really want or don't want. Sometimes it only happens after they are married: they then realise they have done the wrong thing, but it is too late then. I know now that I am gay, and that gives me a certain security. But I wasn't ready to admit that to myself until I was well into my twenties.'

Gulshan, in his twenties, also had an English-language education in a private school, and is from a well-to-do family. 'I knew I was gay when I was about thirteen or fourteen; at least, I knew I was attracted to men, although I did not exactly define to myself what that might mean in practice. I am a gay man, and I want to be able to tell that to the world. At the moment I don't tell the world, because I'm alone and not very secure.'

Sachin is nineteen, from a rich family. His father has a high position in the Planning Commission. He is the youngest of the family, his two older sisters are married. As the only boy, he has been the apple of his parents' eye. He could not possibly tell them he is gay; and although he identifies as gay, he is sure that he also likes girls. He will marry eventually 'for the sake of the family'.

During the months I visited the Park, I became aware that becoming gay or, rather, becoming aware of being gay is an organic process. More men in India are seeing themselves and their lives reflected in this idea, and the individual testimonies often gave a hint of the evolution within people's lives of that consciousness.

Ram Singh, who is thirty-three and in the air force, is based in Shillong in Meghalaya. Between the ages of eighteen and twenty-seven he was, he says, very unhappy: 'This affected my whole life and work. I could not concentrate on studying. I was depressed all the time. There was no friend to talk to, no one with whom to share what I thought was a sickness – this attraction to men. I know now that it is not a sickness; but I also know that if it is denied, it becomes one.

'My family was poor. I went into the air force because I had no prospect of work and couldn't study. I knew I was intelligent, but could not commit myself to passing exams. I went away from home because I knew there was something about myself that I had to discover, and which I could only find in relationships with others. I only knew I was different, and there was something waiting to express itself from within.

'Many Indian men are now finding that they are gay. With Western films, yes and even Western pornography, they see things which they never understood before. The older generation knows nothing of this. Even now, in the villages, relationships are very traditional. Only in the cities, it is all changing, and this new awareness is coming. From my own experience, I can say that it is very frightening.'

Mowla Ao is from Nagaland, a section officer in the Ministry of Agriculture. He is thirty-one, with the pale skin and elongated eyes of hill people. He lives with his sister in south Delhi. He speaks Ao, which is the language of the dominant tribe in Nagaland. After doing his BA in economics in Manipur, he came to Delhi as part of the government quota of jobs reserved for Scheduled Tribes.

Mowla's parents are both dead. He has three brothers and one sister, but a whole network of 'cousin brothers and sisters'. He has come to recognise himself as gay, 'although I do not quite know what it means. I am still confused. I like women also, but mostly I like men. I never knew anyone from Nagaland who is gay until I came to Delhi. . . . If I am gay or not, I do not know what this means. . . . I always knew that I was an Ao, but gay I did not know. Maybe I had to come to Delhi to find this part of who I am.'

Gulshan, twenty-four, knew that he liked men 'since the age of ten or eleven': 'But I did nothing about it until I was in college at the age of eighteen. There were opportunities in college, but you had to be careful to choose the right person or your reputation would be lost and you would be tormented by the others. The ones who were obviously gay you had to avoid, because they had a hard time. I did have one friend who was very effeminate, and – to my shame – I always made sure I was not seen with him in public. We used to go to Delhi Ridge or Buddha Garden, where no one knew us. There was one boy in college who tried to kill himself because he was made to suffer. He was very weak and girlish, and he couldn't stand being laughed at. After he had tried to kill himself, they mocked him because he couldn't even do that successfully.'

Gopinath is thirty-one. Of Nepalese origin, he was born in Megh-alaya, where his family lives. He works in one of the biggest hotels in Delhi. He has four brothers and two sisters. His father was in the army and died in 1987; his mother died four years later.

'I used to be ashamed of being gay. I was sexually abused from the age of eight by a neighbour. Maybe I should be grateful to him for showing me how to be gay, but I did not enjoy it at the time. . . . I am not now ashamed. I would come out, but not at work, because that might damage my chances of promotion, destroy my hopes of becoming captain. . . . I do not know if I will ever marry. If I find Mr Right I may; I will not marry a woman, even though family pressure is there.

'To be gay in India is very difficult. It is a colonial law, which your country left to us. The government of free India also does not think its citizens sufficiently adult to choose their partners. Of course, the law is not often used, but it still creates a sense of something forbidden.'

Rajesh, twenty-seven, is enthusiastically gay. He lives with his parents who, although his friends visit regularly, are insulated from the awareness of their son's homosexuality by their own profound absorption in their Bengali culture, their family and their religion. Rajesh says: 'Most men in Delhi do not know what is gay. The poor and the lower class, they will do it, they are close. They know what is friendship, and they know that this can sometimes become sex. They will see it only as discharge, even if they enjoy. They will not see it as wrong, they will not speak of it, and for them it does not exist. Sex with a man is an expression of friendship only, for them. Of course, it may be that one man enjoys more than the other, but they will pretend it is a substitute for a woman. Most people do not examine their feelings about such things.

'Homosexuality is only what intellectual and cultivated people call it. For me, a man must be talented, intelligent and rich. I like to dance, I love Kathak dancing. I like music and parties. There are three kinds of men-to-men sex in Delhi: need [when men really prefer men]; timepass [men who will accept men when there is nothing else available] and livelihood [when men sell sex for a living.]'

The feeling that India is passing through a time of transition in sexual attitudes was emphasised by Mangesh, a teacher in his forties who comes to the Park. He is a perceptive observer. Speaking of his students, he said: 'I have studied psychology, even though my subject is literature. I have seen how the young people of India have changed in the past twenty years. There is a revolution knocking at India's door, which the older generation cannot recognise. Parents cannot speak to their children, nor children to their parents. The media, economic liberalisation, the opening of India to the world have caused all this. Not everything is bad that comes in, but I cannot even begin to talk to the young people I teach. Some of them are very attractive people. They are drawn to each other. I see evidence of sexual attraction between them, I can see relationships developing, but of such things, of course, I do not speak. But the generations now in power cannot even begin to respond to this. They are still stuck in old hierarchies and habits. We are growing a generation of people who will be strangers to us, just as we are to them. It is like seeing a foreign culture grow at the very heart of what is familiar and traditional.'

Sachin, a nineteen-year-old student, said, 'I talk about being gay at college. We can do this now, so things are changing. A number of students speak openly about their sexual feelings. I have many friends who are girls, and there is no inhibition about open friendships, where I represent no sexual threat to them. This is new in India.'

Karim, retired from Lucknow University, makes a direct connection between the nascent gay movement in Delhi and consumerism. He says, 'It is a direct consequence and symptom of the growth and development of the market economy. They are well off. They feel secure; they have wanted for nothing. They have expressed their wishes and desires for whatever they have wanted, and when it comes to sexuality, they see no reason to be thwarted. They spend their money on clothes, cars, going for parties and discos in private houses. They are imitative of a Western phenomenon in their gay lifestyles as in other aspects of their lives. This should not surprise us. I do not say that I welcome this, because it is something quite alien to our culture and tradition. And by that, I do not mean it is foreign to our marriage and family customs, I mean it is alien to the Indian tradition of same-sex relationships. We have a long and rooted history of men who not only have sex with but also love other men. Why do we need the West to show us how to do it?'

Keshav is one of the few gay men who made being gay sound joyful. He also had a strong sense of irony: 'I am not afraid to say I'm gay. It is a good life. We have fun. We roam around all over Delhi. You never know who you'll meet next. People think Delhi is narrow-minded and puritanical, but beneath the surface it's a lot of fun.

'In college, there was one boy I was crazy about. One day, I got him into my room, and he seemed willing. I took him and kissed him, and we sat down on the floor, kissing and making love until suddenly I discharged into my pants. That was my first introduction to actual physical contact. But we became good friends. I still love him. Since then I've become a little more competent in these matters.'

It is noticeable that all the men who spoke of being gay are influenced by metropolitan life, by English-language education. Some of them have relatives abroad. Two had been to the United States; one to Europe. Their lives are far more open to influences from abroad than are those of the majority of men who have sex with men, many of whom did not see their sexual behaviour as a major determinant of their sense of self.

IV

While my main effort was concentrated on the range and diversity of sexual practices of men cruising in Delhi, particularly in the Park, it is impossible to ignore those more obviously on the margins of Indian society: *hijaras*, transsexuals and transvestites, as well as the even more severely stigmatised – paedophiles. They are all visible in one way or another, even conspicuous, in Delhi; and although their experiences do not fall within the scope of this book, the following brief notes are intended only to signal my recognition of their significance to any discussion of Indian sexualities, both open and covert.

There are a few *hijaras* who visit the Park regularly; they tend to associate with the *khotis*. Some men find it psychologically easier to have sex with a *hijara* than with a man, and even easier than with a *khoti*, who assumes 'feminised' behaviour. Of course, the *hijara* is a familiar figure in Indian social lore, commonly believed to steal male children and castrate them as a source of replenishment for the caste. For the most part, they are feared and stigmatised. It was not always so. They formerly had a function, even if a negative one: they were endowed with powers to ward off misfortune. Now their social role has been degraded, and many are little more than menacing beggars, clapping their hands and holding out a palm to young lovers or newlyweds, the threat lying in their capacity to curse those who do not give.

Many *hijaras* came from the lowest castes, males who, in another context, might have been what is recognised in the West as gay. Sometimes, particularly if unable to produce children, they may have been punished, abandoned by their families, particularly if the male genitalia were not developed, were malformed or rudimentary. Since there was no opportunity for such people to be integrated into the family structure, they became the visible embodiment of a third sex, outside, marginalised, but paradoxically part of the landscapes of orthodoxy and conformism. Their apartness lent them powers of insight and the ability to bless and to curse; they became objects of superstitious respect.

Dilkhush is about thirty. She comes to the Park most days. She has a sweet manner and dresses in vibrant colours that set off the darkness of her skin. Unlike many of her companions, she is married. Her husband is a skilled embroiderer, doing intricate *zari* work – elaborate gold and silver borders on saris and shawls – who can make an income of up to ten thousand rupees a month. The fact that she is married is further illustration of the amorphous sexuality of men: her husband sees in her all that he needs. According to Dilkhush, her sexual ambiguity wedded to his sexual ambiguity produces a happy couple. She begs in the Park; sometimes gives oral sex for a few rupees. She would like to work, but no one will employ a *hijara*. There are, she says, no reservations for *hijaras*, no quotas of government employment. She came to Delhi from her native Lucknow because her indeterminate gender was an embarrassment to her parents and their families. She has had two operations, which together cost almost twenty thousand rupees; but she insists that she is happy with a husband who has no desire for what she calls 'a full woman'. They live in a two-room set in Transyamuna, and no one bothers them. She lives her life as a woman, the neighbours treat her as one; and this has been her ambition since childhood.

'I was trapped in the wrong body. When I had the male part of me removed, this drew away all the male blood that was in me. It was a purification and a liberation. In the place where we live, I am accepted. But people in the streets of Delhi see me, and sometimes they stare or they laugh, the young men especially. But even those young men who mock, they will find an excuse to leave their companions and they come after me. In the Park, I can find some space with the men here, who do not criticise, they do not ask questions.

'It is a curse. When a *hijara* dies, at the funeral, the other *hijaras* beat the corpse and spit on it. This is to thank God that the curse of this life in the shadows is ended for one of us and in the hope of some happier incarnation next time.'

Dilkhush gives the lie to those who say that *hijaras* are from the poorest sections of society. Her family have a house near Lucknow, and they own forty *bighas* of land. They are, however, a very traditional family. It may be that the tradition of the *hijara* is determined culturally rather than economically. Dilkhush says she has no idea about that.

Pushpa has a handsome face, large hands and feet; she wears a cerise-coloured sari and floral-shaped gold earrings. She works part of the west quadrant around India Gate. She is thirty-two and comes from Madras. She came to Delhi, rejected by her parents when it became clear to them that she was not developing properly, as the boy they believed her to be ought to have done.

'When I was small, it did not matter, because you cannot tell from the genitals of a little boy. I worked around the house; I had my tasks. My parents had a grocery store. I was useful. I was loved. I was registered as a boy. My penis was always very small, and when I came to puberty, it did not develop. As I grew older, it did not function. It would not become hard.

'At twenty, I went to hospital to have it removed. This is my destiny, what can I do about it? There is no happiness, I must not even think of it. I live with three others in one room in Karol Bagh, for which we each pay five hundred rupees a month. Here, I have to pay the police. It is not a fixed sum, regular; but whenever they see us, they take whatever we have. I never carry much money, so I lose only the money I have taken in one day.

'I used to be attracted to men. I wanted a boyfriend. I used to have sex with them, but I stopped. They do not treat us well. They only want us for fucking. You cannot have any kind of relationship, any affection, any love from them. They despise us. They will have sex with us only because they cannot get a woman.

'I would like someone to care for me, but I have given up hope of finding such a thing. We live by begging. No one will give us employment. We used to be thought of as bringers of good fortune. Now people give to us only because they are afraid. Maybe if they don't give, they think we have the power to make their children like us. Some believe that we kidnap boys and castrate them; and there are people like me who threaten parents if they will not give us money. But it does not often happen. We are from ordinary families, we all had a mother and father like everyone else; but it is difficult to live as a normal human being in India. I have two brothers and two sisters. I go home occasionally, but they are embarrassed when I visit. My life is here in Delhi now.'

'Faridha' – an assumed name – is from Chennai. He is in his mid thirties, chairman of a major finance company in South India. He is a prominent person in the city, with a high-powered and exacting job, to which he is devoted. His secret, which no one knows, is that he sees himself as, and feels himself to be, a woman. But he has no one to recognise this reality. No one perceives the woman in him, a predicament which is exacerbated by the aggressive male role his work imposes upon him. Indeed, if he had sought the most effective disguise he could conceive, he could scarcely have been more successful.

At home, he sits in his superior apartment overlooking Marina Beach, under the spectacular pyrotechnics of the breaking October monsoon, sheet lightning and streaming rain blurring the city lights through the glass. He dresses mainly in the Western style, wearing dresses, slacks and blouses, with wig and full make-up. (This is itself a significant and self-conscious gesture to a culture that he believes to be more tolerant than his own.) He looks at himself in the glass, wishing he were looking into the eyes of a male lover who will see him as the glamorous attractive and yielding woman he believes himself to be.

When he comes to Delhi, he goes out freely in female dress. If he does this at home – as occasionally happens – he does so in great trepidation, heart pounding, half daring the world to recognise him, yet terrified that they may do so. He has taken drugs to develop his breasts and thinks of himself – his private self, that is – entirely as a woman.

The world of finance is macho, competitive and hard. No more dramatic contrast could be imagined. At work, he conforms to what is expected in the world of finance. He is abrasive, outgoing and tough, and no one suspects what has become a kind of institutionalised schizophrenia in his life. When he dresses as a woman, everything changes – gestures, walk, facial expression, voice. His feminine voice is high-pitched, girlish, with a slight foreign accent. 'I need a boyfriend. I want love. I need to be loved. I know that I have got myself into a career and a way of life in which what I most want in the world is almost impossible.'

Faridha has known since childhood that he identifies completely as a woman; but when he was young, it remained vague, diffuse, not expressed clearly. As time has gone by, it has become more focused, more insistent; until his loneliness is acute – almost, he says, unbearable. Yet he is committed to the most uncompromising of male worlds; a compensation for and an escape from the identity which his high profile all over South and East India forbids him to express. He has never had any sexual experience; only the lonely fantasies and the unsatisfactory auto-eroticism of dressing up for no one but himself.

✿

India Gate. Under the ceremonial arch which dominates the long straight road to the government administrative buildings – a vista lined by ashoka trees, half-swallowed in the gathering mist of an October evening – the red sunset stains the red sandstone of an old, long-cancelled imperial dream. In front of India Gate there are two rectangular expanses of water, in which children sometimes swim and bathe, especially in the hot season. The water is not very clean; but even tonight in the tepid air, there are groups of children, between the ages of seven and sixteen, their sleek bodies glistening as they leap in and out of the ornamental pools.

There are a few foreigners, tourists, taking photographs, no doubt most of them doing so innocently. A few men are dawdling to watch the children swim. Some are more intent than others on observing the young people. A man pretends to chase them. They jump in the water to escape him, laughing and shouting. He leaps in after them, catches them, plays with their wriggling bodies in the turbid water. Some of the boys are naked, apparently unaware of the attentions of adults; although some are clearly performing for the benefit of the spectators. One man – who says he is a rickshaw driver – approaches lone foreigners. He asks them what they want. He can arrange a quiet place. He is clearly a procurer for paedophiles.

One foreigner, a corpulent man in his forties, is sitting on the grass beside the water. He wears wide shorts; his legs are apart and he is clearly without underpants, because some of the boys gather, giggle, point and stare. He offers them some money before taking pictures of them as they leap in and out of the water.

Here, it seems, there is a thriving paedophile trade, carried out in the heart of Delhi, in the very shadow of the national shrine. The children here are nobody's children, street children, anybody's children. This traffic cannot be unknown to the authorities, occurring in such a conspicuous place. But clearly there is no will to stop it. Maybe the police are making money.

Unmesh is a student from near Varanasi. He is doing a computer course in Delhi, which his parents are paying for. A slight young man of twenty-two, he insists that he is not interested in homosex. He finds men wanting sex with men repulsive. What he does like, however, he says, is to be sucked by young boys of fourteen or fifteen, who, he says, are 'charming'. Schoolboys sometimes come to the Park in the afternoon, and, from time to time, they will oblige him. Afterwards, he gives them ten or twenty rupees. He is quite vehement in his denunciation of men who have sex with men and seeks to distance himself from the category, even though popular opinion might judge what he does as far more reprehensible. 'No,' he says emphatically, 'many of the boys like it. They know everything there is to know. Three of them came with me into the jungle one day. They are very happy, and practically fighting with each other to have a go. They thought it was a great game.' Unmesh says he has been doing this since his own childhood. '*Usmen kya nuks hai*? Children enjoy.' I persisted, 'But surely, you must know that you are more mature than they are? You have an understanding which they do not have.' 'I do not make anyone do anything against his wishes. I do not compel them.' Unmesh is petulant and impatient of criticism. He still identifies himself as an adolescent. 'I am not much elder than they. They are my friends. You do not know what is friendship in India.'

V

I have made the distinction between those who say they like 'to enjoy' with men and those who say they want sex with men not simply because the former is a euphemism for the latter, but because it also suggests less of a commitment to a sexual preference for men. Similarly, those who talk of coming to the Park in search of 'homosex' are making a statement that carries a very different emotional charge from those who positively identify themselves as gay.

Specifically, 'to enjoy' implies a casual and almost detached attitude:

I can take it or leave it. This is, however, only partly true. 'Enjoyment' also shades into 'play' or 'fun', which are equally familiar descriptions of what the men say they want. The words *maza, maasti* and *khel* are often invoked – simply playing around. Both enjoyment and play also suggest something set apart from ordinary life: a somewhat more palpable version of dreaming – the night-shrouded clandestinity which many prefer – but still abstracted from reality, distant from daily necessity.

One day, in another Delhi park, I am sitting in the shadow of one of the half-neglected red sandstone Mogul tombs which are to be found surrounded by grazing cattle and echoing with the cries of playing children. It is early evening. A young man comes and sits on the steps of the tomb. His name is Mohamad Azmi. He is eighteen and works as a mechanic, mending punctures and retreading tyres. He lives with his maternal uncle and family in Hauz Khas. He tells me about his village in Uttar Pradesh, his family, how he has come to Delhi to look for better opportunities for making money. He is an attractive young man, with a mass of dark curly hair and a wide smile. But what he really wants to talk about is sex. He asks questions about the West that by now have become familiar. Can you see blue films? At what age do young people have sex? He asks if I have any pictures of naked women or men. He thinks he may be abnormal because he wants sex so much. He cannot stop thinking about it. When he stands up, his penis is erect through the oil-stained trousers. Sometimes, he says, he comes here 'to play'. He says that talking about it always makes him feel sexy. Since there are no girls available, he says, he sometimes plays with men.

This insistence on play easily merges into the response of those who claimed they only do it for relief (or discharge, as they sometimes say). For them, they often declare, this is second best, and if they were married or if they had access to women, they would not even contemplate such an activity. Of course, this dissociation of themselves may cover a multitude of felt responses. Most of the men appeared to feel more secure, sheltered from a culture of shame, if they could place themselves at a remove from what they actually do. If even their own behaviour is thus distanced from them, how much more remote must be any sense of essential identity through sexual activity.

Those who say they do it for money are also setting themselves emotionally apart from their actions. Some of these, however, did say they enjoyed it. 'I wouldn't do it if I didn't like it,' said one young man, while another was anxious to let it be known that he did it solely because he was unemployed and added that if he had a proper job, he would not think of coming here.

In one sense, my very presence in the Park, and my desire to talk with the men about what they did, falsifies the phenomenon I am trying to discuss. It is not within the Indian experience to rationalise or even to name sex between men; so to describe what people actually do, rather than what they say they do, is itself an almost impossible task. Once named, it soon becomes something alien; the word *gay* simply mystified the great majority of the men in the Park. To do it but not to talk of it leaves it in an acceptable penumbra, so that it can be, in some measure, integrated into the lives of individuals, like a familiar landscape seen at twilight: the contours are there, but the details cannot be discerned in the gathering dark.

Some of the questions I asked, therefore, had to be oblique. Perhaps the most significant of all was at what age, and in what circumstances, they became aware of their attraction to men; connected to this was the question of who initiated them. By posing it like this, I hoped to gain a sense of the dawning consciousness, the moment when awareness could no longer be denied. So I asked, 'At what age did you know you wanted to have sex with men?' This was the response:

'Ever since I can remember', or *'bachpan se'* (from childhood): 5
Below the age of 10: 3
Age 10–11: 3
Age 12–13: 8
Age 14–16: 8

Age 17–18:	13
Age 19–21:	11
Age 22–25:	10
Age 26–30:	4
Over 30:	3
Didn't say:	7

There are some surprises here. Slightly over 25 per cent said they knew they wanted to have or had had sex with men, below the age of thirteen. On the other hand, almost as many – 23.7 per cent – were not even aware of what they wanted until they were twenty-two or older. The most extreme case was a man in his fifties who discovered his liking for men only when he was over forty.

'I was in my early forties. One day, I was at a *mela* [a fair], and a large crowd had gathered around a juggler and an acrobat. As the people pressed closer to see what was happening, I became aware of a man in front of me, who was standing with his hands clasped behind his back. As the crowd pushed me forward, I felt him groping for my genitals. I was surprised that I found this exciting, and I had an erection, although nothing was further from my mind at the time. He turned round and beckoned to me to follow him. We went to some wild jungly place, and that was the first time I learned to enjoy with a man. I was disturbed by this. You do not know yourself. You think you are a mature man, and you have lived long enough to know everything that happens in your life. Then one day you are brought to face something which you did not even suspect. I have four children: the oldest two at university, the two younger ones still at school. It turns your life upside down. I still have barely come to terms with it, even though since that time, I have looked to repeat this experience whenever I have the opportunity.'

For many of those who said they have always known what they wanted, the early experience was relatively untroubled. But a minority found it distressing and unwelcome, particularly those who had been abused as children or adolescents. Peter first knew he was gay from a relationship with a teacher, to whose house he used to go for tuition in mathematics.

'One night, it was raining very heavily. I had made up my mind that I would not go for coaching. But the thought of staying at home in the rain was very boring. I didn't particularly enjoy tuitions, but the prospect of going seemed more interesting than sitting at home. During the lesson, the rain came on very fast, and the streets became flooded. My teacher suggested I should not go home that night. He telephoned my parents, to tell them he thought it would be unwise to send me home in the rain. So I slept with him. It didn't surprise me that he expected me to sleep in his bed. That night, we had sex. It was very painful; but in spite of that I knew this was what I wanted. I was thirteen. Afterwards, it became easier. And we continued like that for a long time. There was no suspicion, because I was going for tuition. He was very kind to me. Later, he married and now has two children. But even after his marriage, whenever I went home I would go to see him, and he would arrange for us to be alone. We continued to have sex. Now it has stopped, but I know that he still loves me very much, and I certainly love him. This has been very precious to me, and it still is.'

Arun was sexually abused by a neighbour from the age of eight. 'I knew it was wrong, but I never said anything to anyone. Perhaps I felt that I would be held responsible if I spoke out; but in any case, it was part of the normal way of things that adults could do as they wished with children. To some extent this is still true in India. No one will believe a child who accuses an adult of such a thing.'

Pandu is now twenty-seven. A handsome man, almost pretty, slight. He is from a village near Hubli in Karnataka and works in Delhi in a shelter for the destitute run by an international charity. 'I come from a family of five – three boys and two girls. I knew I liked men from the age of ten or eleven. When I was eleven, I went to have extra tuitions with my teacher, who was then unmarried and living alone in Hubli.

'This man used to kiss and fondle me. It wasn't really a sexual relationship at that age. I derived great comfort from his attention. Since he was living close to the school, he asked permission that I should go and live with him. My parents agreed. From that time, I shared the teacher's life and slept with him every night.

'By the time I was thirteen or fourteen, the teacher started to want something more. He asked if he might penetrate me. I said yes, but I was not quite sure what that might mean. It was a very painful and traumatic experience. I didn't like it. After he had finished, I just lay there with my eyes closed, without moving. Actually I was in a state of shock. He became frightened and thought he had seriously injured me. I remained like that for a whole day and a night.

'Later, he did it again. Slowly, I learned to relax and to enjoy. He was my regular partner for many years. He remains my good friend. . . . He has since married and has two children, boys. He still tells me that he loves me very much. Whenever I go home, I always go to see him. I am grateful to him, because he taught me what love is.'

The story of initiation by a teacher is not uncommon. At least four men mentioned a teacher as a significant figure; and although they were introduced to sex before they were physically ready for it, all nevertheless remembered these men with affection.

Pandu added, 'No one in the village or in Hubli suspected that the teacher might be sheltering me for any other reason than out of charity, the kindness of his heart. They might have thought he would be less lonely if I stayed with him, but they would never have dreamed that this might involve sex. This attitude is now changing in India. People who took care of the young used to be thought of as giving something voluntarily to young people. Now things are different. Such things still happen, especially in the rural areas, but now people would be suspicious if a man wants to take a pupil into his home. They would now ask, "What does he want to do that for?" and even though people's minds might not run to sex straight away, they might suspect his reasons; they might think he is trying to get money from the boy's parents.'

A recurring theme in the story of the awakening of consciousness is the individual who made the approach, who showed the narrators what it meant, who revealed to them the pleasure to be derived from their own bodies. There is an undertow of blame running through many of the testimonies. It is almost as though the men are saying 'If it had not been for this person, I would never have known what it was to have sex with men.' There is a powerful sense of an other, an external agency, an older person, a stranger or foreigner doing the work of initiation; and this serves to exculpate the individual from responsibility for his own sexuality. Sometimes it comes across as if it had happened to someone else, a strong sense of dissociation. There is a persistent feeling that the person recounting the story has not had this experience at all. It remains outside; it took place in a dream, in the darkness, in secret. Perhaps only by banishing it to the margin of experience can it be truly integrated into life.

Mohinder, twenty-five, is from Kanpur. One of three brothers, he has come to Delhi to look for work so that his siblings may continue their studies. Until now, his whole life has been spent in study: a BA in commerce, a diploma in environment and ecology which he did by correspondence from Delhi, English typing skills, and then a course in computer skills in Kanpur. Mohinder came to Delhi full of hope, confident that his efforts would earn him a job. He has been here for two or three months and has already received much unwelcome instruction in the crowded job-market for graduates. He carries his biodata in a neat plastic wallet. He says, 'I thought it would be easy to find work in Delhi. I didn't know that everyone else has also done computer studies. Many also know English much better than I do.'

When Mohinder came to Delhi, he came to lodge with a cousin of his father. This man, who is in his thirties and works in a plastics factory, had been urging him for some time to try his luck in Delhi, inviting him to stay with him in the room he rents in Moti Bagh. Family pressure finally drove Mohinder to accept: his father is much older than his mother and recently had a stroke. He can no longer work, and the two brothers are fourteen and seventeen, both anxious to continue their studies.

'My cousin was very welcoming. He said it would be company for him to have me there. He has a wife and two children who live in a village five kilometres from ours near Kanpur. He sees them only at Diwali. The room is not very big. There is a kitchen and a bathroom that is shared with the other people who live on the same floor of the building. There is only one bedroll on the floor. My cousin invited me to share it with him on the first night. I hesitated, but the floor was cold, so I accepted. He put his arm round me, and it felt good. I was secure. I felt protected. I do not like to sleep alone – I have always slept with my brothers.

'After some little time, I could feel his cock through the lunghi I wear. I tried to make a distance between him and me, but he followed me. He lifted up my lunghi and tried to penetrate me. I was very frightened, because he is elder to me, and I have always looked up to him. And then not only is he my father's relative, but he had invited me to stay in his room without paying any rent. I thought it best to let him do as he wanted. I was very uncomfortable. It was unpleasant, but I did not stop him from doing.

'I thought I didn't like it. I said he must never do that again. There was some blood. He said he was sorry. But the next night, he did it again. I didn't stop him. I don't know why. I thought, well, maybe this is what I have to do if I am to stay here with him without paying money. After a few days, I came to feel that it was good. I began to enjoy.

'He showed me this place. I come to sit before I go for interview for a job. Sometimes I go into the jungle with army men. They give me fifty rupees. One army officer gave me two hundred rupees. It makes me a little independent. I do not have to ask my father for money. I never heard of this in the village. I still feel shame, but I enjoy.'

Nataranjan, twenty-eight, had his first experience of sex at thirteen. 'It was the time of a wedding. One of the guests who had travelled far came to sleep in our house. I shared a bed with him. The first night, he took my hand and placed it over his cock, which was hard. I did not understand what was happening. Next night, he did the same thing. He moved my hand back and forward along his penis until I felt this strange stickiness. The third night, he told me, "Turn over", and he penetrated me. It was painful and I was shocked. I have never wanted to be penetrated since that time, although I like sex with men.'

A notable feature of the testimonies is the role of weddings in sexual discovery, and not merely for the principal protagonists. The story is that relatives, often distant cousins – that is, virtual or actual strangers – come to stay for the period of the wedding and share a bed with the young man. A version of this occurred five or six times, too frequently to be coincidental. There are obvious reasons why such occasions should provide an opportunity for sex. For one thing, there is a heightened sense of excitement at the time of a wedding. Something of the eroticism of the event is contagious. Everyone knows its purpose is for sexual consummation, and something of this feeling catches up many young men in its forbidden exaltations. It may be that the fantasies they entertain are of women, but that is not the point; younger boys and young men, who find the unfamiliar warmth of a stranger in their beds, are available. There is also a strong feeling that the atmosphere of excitement serves as a kind of alibi: it was not the real me, it was the intoxication of the celebration, the dancing, sometimes the unfamiliar taste of alcohol, that led to this discovery.

Mahesh, who is twenty, discovered sex at the time of a wedding, when some relatives had come to the village. 'One man slept in my bed, and he roused me in the night to have sex with me. I was half asleep. I was thirteen. It was like a dream, and the next day, I did not know whether it had happened or if I had only imagined it. That fellow went away after the wedding, and I never met him again; but from that day I knew that I wanted to have sex with men.'

Javed, who grew up in Delhi, also learned what he wanted at a wedding. 'I was twenty-one. Some people had come from the village to our house. There was a marriage party, and my mother said I would have to share my bed with a cousin, a man I did not know. A marriage is a time when everybody gets excited, especially all the young men. They are dancing and eating, and everyone feels very free and happy. I think both this man and I had become very excited by all the celebration. I kept looking at him as he was dancing, and I kept thinking, Oh, I shall be sleeping with him tonight. He had a lot of hair that moved up and down as he danced, and his eyes were shining. Once or twice, he caught my glance and smiled, and I thought my heart would stop. I found myself wondering what he would look like without any clothes on, how he would smell, whether he would touch me. When he looked at me, I had to lower my eyes, I felt shame and I could feel that I was blushing. I felt like a girl. When the time came to go to bed, I was embarrassed. We lay in the darkness talking about the wedding. I could see his penis was standing under the *chador* but I didn't dare touch him. Then he kissed me on the lips and it took my breath away. I was very responsive, and it was through him that I learned to enjoy.

'Before that day, I had no idea. It was like waking up. The next day he had to go home. I walked around, it was like parting for ever. I wanted him to go, because I thought afterwards that I hated him for making me do this thing. Then when he had gone I kept walking around and saying "I like this thing, what does it mean?" After he'd gone, I felt I had lost someone very dear to me. I cried. I've never met him from that day. But I am grateful to him, because he opened my eyes to something I had not seen.'

Harsh is twenty and works in a garment factory. He has 'done sex', as he puts it, with two relatives, both cousins, who had come from the village to the house where he stays. 'They never spoke about it afterwards. They did it, but they denied it. No, they didn't even deny, because for them they never really did it. It happened without them knowing. But I knew, because I saw they had an erection, I felt it. I wanted to say something, but I soon came to see that it was better if I keep silent.'

Jaspal is eighteen. He discovered sex two years ago, when a relative came to stay with the family in their village close to Jaipur. This man, a 35-year-old, had come for a wedding. He shared his bed: 'I was excited by the idea of sleeping with him. I went to sleep with his arm holding me, and I felt very happy and safe. Then I woke up and found he was trying to enter me. I did not like it. I do not like to be penetrated. I protested, and he stopped. The next morning he didn't say anything.'

One man said he had sex with the bridegroom on the day before the wedding. 'He was three years younger than I. I was staying with him and his family, and in the afternoon before the wedding, we went for a walk into the forest. I had been married for a year. He wanted to talk to me about sex, because he said he knew nothing and was afraid. We went into a quiet place, and he asked me to tell what it was like, what would be expected of him. Then he asked me to show him. I found all the talk of sex quite exciting, and I was in a state of arousal. Then we did, and I came to know that he had enjoyed many times since he was at school. He said he was afraid of making love to his wife and did not know if he would be able to do it with the enthusiasm that was expected of him. He has since come to Delhi, and we are good friends. He does not speak of that incident, and he now has three children. I enjoy with men and women equally, and I think he feels the same.'

There are other stories of how awareness comes. The Delhi buses appear in these a number of times, as do bus stands and Maruti cars (always a Maruti, never an Ambassador; the Maruti is a symbol of wealth and power, a form of transport that is taking India into the future). Chance encounters with foreigners, usually Westerners, figure with some prominence. But perhaps the most startling example of a man trying to shed responsibility for his sexual activity was the man who blamed it on the size of his penis. Bharat, a small man in his forties, is adamant that his need for sex comes from the fact that he has a big cock: 'I am only a small man, but my cock is eight inches. It is very thick and strong. It has a *til* [a mole], which is lucky. This is why I must have sex often. My wife cannot satisfy, but she does not know and I do not speak to her of it. I am endowed with much sexual energy, I do not know why.'

Of the more usual places of initiation, one most frequently mentioned is on Delhi buses.

Dinesh is twenty-four, a mechanic at Palam airport. His work is to check the aircraft on the runway before departure. He is a very handsome man, with striking greenish eyes, pale skin and crimson lips which part readily in a smile. He is from Gorakhpur in Uttar Pradesh, where his wife and children live. The family has ten *bighas* of land (about two acres). Dinesh stays alone in a small rented room at Palam. It was only a little over a year ago that he discovered he liked sex with men.

'In the bus one day, a man sat next to me who told me he was an employee of the Bank of India. I did not know why he was sitting so close. I thought perhaps it was because the bus was so crowded, and people were leaning over us to hold on to the rail. There is never enough space in the bus at busy times of day. His hand was holding the edge of the seat, and as the bus jerked, he slid it under my leg. I tried to move away, but his hand followed me.

'I got off the bus, and I saw that he too was getting down at the same stop. I walked on, and it soon became clear that he was following me. He stopped when I did and began to walk whenever I moved on. He invited me to drink tea at his house. I hesitated. My heart was beating rather fast, because I knew there was something else behind the invitation, although I could not imagine what it was. I knew something was going to happen. His family were not at home. He gave me a bottle of Kingfisher beer, which I do not usually drink. After this, my head was swimming. I thought maybe he had placed some drug in it. He began to take off my clothes. I did nothing to stop it. I enjoyed.'

Jain is from Madurai in Tamil Nadu. He is twenty-eight, working for the Union Government, supplying stationery for offices. He lives with a colleague in a single room, for which they each pay five hundred rupees a month. Jain has been married for five years; he has a daughter who is three. His wife and child came to Delhi to be with him, but his wife was unhappy here. Delhi was cold, his wife cannot speak Hindi, and she missed her family. They went back to Madurai, where the family has some land.

'I didn't know anything about sex until marriage. My wife had to teach me what to do. I like sex with her. But it was only when I came to Delhi that I learned about men. Sometimes men stand close to you. I did not like this. I found the intimate contact of other men's bodies disturbing. I used to wait until late in the evening before going home, when there was more space to sit and I would not be touched by others.

'One day, I left work earlier than usual. A man stood next to me. He was holding a plastic bag, and as the bus jolted, this man let his hand touch my crotch. I felt myself react. I was shocked and excited at the same time. The man looked at me, and he moved his head and eyes to suggest that I should follow him. I thought everybody in the bus would be watching, but no one noticed anything. I got off when he did, and he waited for me. We went to his room. The man held me close to him. Then he took off his clothes and I did the same. He drew me onto the bed and touched me with his hands. He did it very slowly and gently, and it was something I had never known before.

'It was very good. He was a nice man. I was very frightened, but I also enjoyed very much. I did not know such things happened. Even less did I know that I would want such things.'

Mowla Ao from Nagaland says, 'I came to Delhi to work when I was twenty-five. The first time I had sex was late one night, when I was waiting for the last bus, not sure whether I had missed it or not.

It was May, very hot. A man came into the bus shelter where I was sitting, and he sat close to me. He put his hand on the seat near to where mine was. I moved away, but he moved closer. I took my hand away and accidentally touched his. I said sorry, but he smiled and said, "No problem." Then I got up. He followed me, and said, "Shall we walk?" I didn't know what was happening. I said, "I'll miss my bus." He said his car was parked nearby. He had a Maruti.

'I went with him to his place. He was very nice. I went for a shower, and he came into the bathroom with me. We washed one another, and then he entered me. I felt some pain and some pleasure. He was very kind. I often think of him. Afterwards, he gave me his phone number, but I never saw him again. I was lucky. What happens to you with your first experience can have a great influence on your life.'

Travel figures largely in sex: this, like play and enjoyment, represents time taken out of daily life; it suggests an elsewhere, places in which normal rules are in abeyance, interstices in time in which anything can happen. Krishna, thirty-one, says, 'I had been in Delhi only two or three weeks when I was picked up from the bus stand by a man on a scooter. He took me to his home in Noida. He told me where to go in Delhi when you want to enjoy.'

Prasad is thirty-three, owner of a garment factory in Okhla that employs twenty-eight workers. The garments are not for export, but go all over India: shirts, trousers, ladies' skirts. Prasad has two children, four and two, and a substantial house in Greater Kailash. He has worked hard and made a success of the business, which his father started and bequeathed to him. He is a plump man, with a pleasant face unmarked by any failure, the image of well-being and contentment. Tomorrow is the day after Diwali, the day on which brothers honour their sisters. He will visit his two sisters, make them gifts and give them money.

'Five years ago, I was travelling to Rajasthan by train. I was going to see a customer about a consignment of garments. At Old Delhi station, I met a man who sat beside me and engaged me in conversation while I was waiting for the train. He sat close to me on the seat, and his arm was behind me along the back of the bench. I became aware of a closeness that was something more than just the way men sit together in public. I became aware that my cock was stirring, and as I looked down I observed that of the stranger was also.

'He asked me to come with him to a small hotel near the station, where it is possible to hire rooms by the hour. We had sex. Since then, I discovered that I have an interest in men. I like to penetrate and to suck. This does not interfere with my relationship with my wife. In any case, she is busy with the children and our home. And I have the factory.'

The Maruti car – emissary of industrialised private mobility – was mentioned by Mowla Ao. It recurred several times; and its owner is also a symbolic figure – someone successful, of superior social standing, usually a prosperous, mature man picking up a younger man – who serves as a justificatory device. 'I was the innocent party in this encounter' is also part of the story.

Balu tells how he was returning home from his job as a security guard outside a posh house in south Delhi: 'A man in a Maruti car stopped and offered me a lift. I accepted. The man parked in a quiet spot and asked for sex. I did as he asked. He gave me one hundred rupees. He wanted to see me again the next day, so I arranged to meet him at the same time. He took me to his room, and this time he gave me two hundred rupees.'

Ajay, twenty, works as a computer operator for an in-flight catering company at the international airport. He earns Rs 1500 a month and lives with his parents in a two-room set at Palam. His father is an engineer with the Delhi Development Authority. 'I was walking home from work one night about six months ago, when a Maruti car stopped. The driver offered me a ride. I accepted, although it was close to my home. He invited me to his house, and said he would like to have sex with me. He gave me two hundred and fifty rupees.'

I had one insight into the point of view of the Maruti drivers. One day, a group of gay-identified men were talking about the fun they had, driving around Delhi at night, offering lifts to young men. The offers were rarely refused, and much of the excitement came from the fact that the young men would rarely be aware of the object of this charity. The amusement arose from talking to the young men about sex, trying to arouse them and then suggesting that they might do it together. Some of course refused, but a surprising number were agreeable to the invitation, which for many proved to be their first experience of sex. Some of the young men were vendors of soft toys or sleeping bags, handkerchiefs, combs, VCR covers, leather wallets; others were late-night strollers.

The discussion made me uncomfortable. It savoured too much of the rich preying on the poor, the sophisticated upon the innocent, the advantaged upon the disadvantaged. When I expressed some of my reservations, they were incredulous. 'It was only a game. We wanted to have some fun.' Yet it was impossible to separate their perception of fun from their sense of the advantage that their superior status gave them. It made them feel completely safe, a measure of the vast social gulfs across which people in India must face each other.

The element of blame attached to whoever initiated the men into sex is nearly always a displacement of responsibility from a younger man towards an elder, even when this is what the younger man wanted. Relatives play a significant role in this: with wide networks of kin, these make up the largest portion of the acquaintance of many young men, and it is scarcely surprising if it is among them that the first partner is found.

Sachin, who is nineteen, had his first sexual experience when he was in Twelfth Standard, when he was seventeen. A relative, an 'uncle', had come to stay from the area in Uttar Pradesh where the family has property. 'He was lying on the bed in my sitting room, and he asked me to come and sit beside him. I did so, innocently, suspecting nothing. He held me close to him and started to take off my clothes. I told him to stop, which he did. Then, in the night, the same thing happened. He asked me to lie beside him. He started again to take off my clothes. Again I asked him to stop, and he did what I asked. I was confused, you know, in the state of wanting it to happen and yet not wanting it. Then I regretted it and moved closer to him. Then we did it. My father has no idea that this happened. I think he knows that such things do exist, but he cannot suspect that I am like that. I hope he will never know. The second time was with a doctor who was in the college where I am studying. He invited me to his house. We kissed, drank some tea, that was all. He said he would call me. The second time I went there we had sex.'

One of the most telling assignments of culpability came from a nineteen-year-old who blamed his educational failure on the fact that he was seduced by a cousin. Rakesh is a very intelligent young man who was expected to do well in his exams. He was devastated by failure and is now doing a correspondence course in education and librarianship. 'I live in Moti Bagh with three sisters and two brothers. My father is an electrician, but for the past eight years, he has been addicted to Brown Sugar [a heroin derivative], and this means that he gives very little to my mother to help keep the family. She gets some money from my two older brothers, who are working.

'I want to be a teacher. Unfortunately, maths is my weak subject, and this is why I failed my exams in the Twelfth Standard. I had to do it again, but I couldn't go to college. I love reading, and I love roaming all over the city. There is no park or public place in Delhi that I do not know. And then I read everything, from *a* to *z*, books, encyclopaedias, newspapers, magazines, stories.

'The real reason why I failed my exam was sex. Just before I was to do the Twelfth Standard exams, my cousin, who is a few years older than I am, came to stay at my home. I shared my bed with him and fell asleep with his body pressing close to mine, and his hand was around me on my stomach. When I woke up, I found he had separated my banyan from my dhoti, and my cock was in his hand. I was very frightened, but I enjoyed it. Afterwards, I woke up again to find him sucking my cock. Every day for a week, we slept together and we did sex every night.

'I think this experience made my brain weak, and this is what caused me to fail. I went to a government school, and I was a good student. All the teachers looked to me to do well. I'm sure that sex like this is a dirty habit. *Samlaingik sambandh* – same-sex relationships – are wrong. I have read in books that this is not shameful, and it is not a sin, but I do not agree. My experience is not like this. Too much sex destroys the brain and makes the body weak. I want to stop this thing, but when you have started, you cannot. Afterwards I feel bad, shame, unworthy. I would not want my brothers or my mother to know what I have done. I believe that the vital force of the body is stored in the head, and each time *pani nikal jata hai* [I come], some weakness occurs. This is why our religion has always taught that abstinence is good. The sages and the holy men gained their moral power through abandoning sexual contact. Gandhiji believed that the ability to overcome sexual desire gave him the strength to keep up the struggle for freedom.'

Rakesh spends much time alone. He bites his nails, does not like the colour of his skin, says that his brothers and sisters are fairer than he is. He does not consider himself good-looking, even though he has a very pleasant face and beautiful eyes.

'See what this has done to me. I cannot find work. I have no work because I have no experience and no experience because I have no work. I have done temporary jobs as peon in an office through an agency, but I have no sustained period in one occupation. I work on my correspondence course for three hours each day, and I go to the school on Sunday which is run for those doing the course.

'I cannot think of telling my family of what happened between me and my cousin, even though it took place at home. I worry about everything. Sometimes I think I hate my cousin for what he did to me, but I do not hate him, and when he comes to stay with me, I want to have sexual relations with him. Afterwards it is myself I hate because I do not have the strength to say no.'

Rajan, thirty, is from Tamil Nadu: 'I had my first experience of sex at twelve or thirteen. I sucked the cock of a cousin. At the time I thought "What's the big deal? Is that it? Is that all it is?" I think I was too young then, I was not ready for it. Later, at eighteen, in a college hostel, I had a more serious relationship that showed me how good it could be. I think that young people are often protected by their own unreadiness for sex, so unless something very violent is done to them, they are penetrated or something, it does not make a great impression on them.'

Rajesh is from a Bengali family who returned to Calcutta after Partition and from there to Delhi, where his father worked in the police department. Rajesh is warm, vivacious, impulsive. At the age of thirteen, he was fucked by a cousin, a man of twenty-six, who was living with the family at the time. 'At first, I was very shocked and surprised. He kept on doing it for two years. The first time, it was very painful, it made me bleed. I thought I had been permanently injured. He did not think of me at all. He was not gay. He was using me only, because he had no woman, and I suppose a thirteen-year-old boy is the best substitute. I could not understand how he could not know how much he was hurting me. One day he even brought his friend home, so that he could have the same enjoyment. He knew I would not tell anyone. It had the effect of making me confused. It was very insensitive. I thought that since he was a member of our family, he ought to be taking care of me. Instead, he was using me. By the age of sixteen, I had boyfriends, but it was only much later that I came to know that I also enjoy sex with women.'

Some of the men mention those from a higher class, a more elevated social position, as having introduced them to sex with men. This is a variant of the familiar boy-seduced-by-teacher story; but in most cases, they were already adults. Manohar's story is characteristic.

Manohar is in his forties. A small thick-set man with grizzled hair, he is a cook in Bihar Bhavan, the official state office in Delhi. He is married with two daughters, who are twelve and ten. He prefers men to women. He loves his wife, although she knows nothing of his preferences.

'She is a village woman. The only thing that women from the village know is intercourse. Most do not even know that until after they are married. They will not touch your cock even with their hands, even less with their mouth. She does not like me to kiss her breasts, and I do not touch her private parts with my hand. Some city women are different, maybe. But for our village women, there is only one form of sex, and one single position. When I go home to my village, if my wife sees me with another woman, I'll be thrown out of the home. If she came to know I was with a man, then I would be beaten up by her family and thrown out as well. . . . Life is like this. I have to keep my desire for men a secret from my family.

'Most of my contacts with men are just for sex. I had one friend, who was my first. I miss him even now.

'One day, a holiday, I had gone to the underground toilets at India Gate. A man followed me. I did not know what had impelled me to go to that place. I did not know it was a place where men meet other men. Something just drove me there. I was in a strange mood, thinking of home, feeling alone in Delhi.

'This man stood next to me. He was very well dressed. He showed me his cock, and I found this exciting. When we got outside, he spoke to me. He was very polite, an educated man. He had his car nearby, and he took me to the place where he lived. A big house in a posh suburb, Defence Colony. We drank some beer and whisky, ate good food, and then he took me to his bed and we had sex.

'He was a senior officer in the Indian Administration Service. His wife also worked for the IAS. She was away. After we had done, we took a bath. Then we drank more alcohol. I like to be active, I do not like the passive role. He was happy with that. Afterwards, we did again, and he asked me to stay the night, which I did.

'He gave me his telephone number and told me to call. Then whenever his wife was away on tour, we could meet. I called him after some time, and he said, "Come and meet me at my house." I said, "I do not know the way," because we had gone by car. He sent his car for me. I visited him from time to time, and it was very nice. I had a great affection for him, and I think he felt the same. It is very sweet to have the time and the privacy to be together, not to hurry, to get to know one another. I had never known of such a thing, and I thought it could go on like this for ever.

'But it became known that he was also having a relationship with someone else, a man who was a principal secretary in Bihar Bhavan itself, the place where I also worked! And he was taking the active role with this man, even though he had told me he was interested only in the passive part. I do not know how this came to be known; I think someone had informed his superiors. They questioned him. They demanded to see his address book. When they found my name, they said, "Who is this?" He said, "He is a cook, a friend of mine." How does it come about that someone in your high position is knowing someone as low as this?" they asked him.

'One thing about homosex is that it brings together people from all parts of society. Only this can unite rich and poor, highest and lowest castes. This makes it appear to be a great threat to those who do not take part in such activities. So they well understood what was happening, even though he denied it, and there was no proof that anything had happened. He said it had all been a rumour by someone anxious to discredit him.

'He was transferred, and then our relationship was finished. It is very hard to maintain a relationship with another man in India, especially if he belongs to a different social world. Social and family pressures leave no space in society for anything else. This is one reason why many men live apart from their families. They leave their wife and children in the village, and they come to Delhi or Mumbai to enjoy. But even here it is still very difficult to meet, to find a secure place, to escape the eyes of people.'

It is not so much that Manohar is blaming his influential friend for having introduced him to sex with men, although he certainly felt betrayed when his friend disappeared without ever contacting him again; but it does place the relationship outside of his real life, in which he does not drink whisky, travel by car or visit Defence Colony. The point about friendships with those from other social classes is that they take place outside of normal expectations; they are not perceived as part of the man's 'real life', which is principally based on family and work and relationships of only casual propinquity, with neighbours and work colleagues.

Amit, an army mechanic in his early thirties, had had no experience of sex with men until he joined the army at the age of nineteen. Soon after entering the services, he attracted the attention of one of the senior officers, who arranged for him to do special duties; and he was soon in attendance as driver and mechanic for this officer, at both official and social functions. On one occasion, when he accompanied his superior out of Delhi on a visit to Rajasthan, he was offered alcohol but refused it.

'Later in the evening, he gave it to me again, and this time I took it. I had never tasted it before, and I did not like it. That night, I was to sleep in a small room close to that of the superior officer. After I had fallen asleep, I woke up to find him getting into my bed. When you are new in the army, you have the idea that you must obey officers under all circumstances. I had been in the service for only four months. I did not think it was right, but I was not strong enough to say so; I was not to know that all officers did not do this with those servicemen they liked. But I enjoyed. After that, he made me go with him on every visit as his driver, and he had sex with me at every opportunity. Until that time, I was a simple village boy. I knew nothing of all this. But once you have been introduced to this activity, you cannot pretend that you are any longer innocent. You cannot return to the way you were.'

The most dramatic form of outsider relationships involves those who meet foreigners – in most cases, Westerners. This distances them even further from the daily life of the Indian men. Sometimes the foreigners are idealised, since they often take the Indians off on brief visits of luxury to hotels, or on trips, giving them a glimpse of the life of the tourist, the casual visitor, the exotic outsider.

'Earlier this year', says Dinesh, who is twenty-four, 'I met an American in Connaught Place. He was staying in the Marina Hotel, where he was paying one hundred and twenty dollars a night. Three times he took me there. He gave me food and drink, and I stayed all night. It was first class. I like white skin. It is more beautiful than ours, which is dark and looks dirty.' Indeed, the foreigner often becomes an object of fantasy, as well as being a beneficiary of the profound inferiorisation of Indians, many of whom express a liking for fair skin, an attraction to Westerners and a conviction that their own colour is unattractive, 'black' or 'too dark'.

I met a forty-year-old, working as a salesman, who had his first experience of sex with a man only one year ago. He says he had taken his mother-in-law to the hospital, the All India Institute of Medical Sciences, where she was to undergo an operation. His wife and two children returned home, while he prepared to stay for the night. During the night, he had sex with a doctor in one side-room. Before that, he says, he had never known sex with a man.

Karan is hovering around India Gate, looking hungrily for someone to pick him up. He looks about fifteen, but when he approaches, he says that his age is seventeen. I am with a friend who works in a government department and who tells me that he has met this boy before. He has been taken up by a number of foreigners. The boy has a small face with regular features, is very slim and self-conscious. His pale blue jeans are grubby, and he looks as though he has been sleeping rough for some time. He asks me if I can find work for him. He says he can do anything – housework, cooking; he does not care, as long as he has a job in a house. As we speak, his story slowly unfolds, although the chronology is difficult to piece together.

He tells how his mother and sister live in Sultanpur in Uttar Pradesh. They are poor, with less than one *bigha* of land. His father, he says, was a taxi-driver, but was killed in a road accident when Karan was very young. He says virtuously that he ran away from home to find work to support his family. He was picked up by a German who took him to Kathmandu. He stayed in the best hotels for three weeks. He was given clothes, good food, comfort, in exchange for sex. When the German left India, he simply dropped the boy.

Later, he says, he was picked up by an official working for the World Health Organization, an American. He was given work by this man, who lived in Jor Bagh with his wife and children. The boy boasts that he used to fuck his employer. He worked as 'cook and assistant' for the family; when his friend was away at work, he says, 'his wife used to suck my cock.' After one year, they went back to the US, and the man gave him three lakh of rupees (about $9000). Karan lived in an apartment, bought clothes, enjoyed life, invited his friends to stay with him and soon spent all the money. Now he is back at India Gate, looking for someone with whom he can repeat this experience.

Impossible to know how much of this is true. But what is certain is that he is sure he has found the key to adult behaviour, the source of his power: sex. I say to him that it would be better for him to go home to Sultanpur rather than hang around India Gate. He says he would rather be at home, but he cannot afford to go back. I give him a hundred rupees. He says, 'The bus fare is one hundred and fifty rupees.' I repeat that this is not a good place, and there is no future for him here.

All of which he readily assents to, but clearly does not agree. A few days later I see him again, this time in Connaught Place. He pretends not to recognise me. Later, we come face to face for a third time.

I say to him, 'You decided not to go home then?' He says balefully, 'I didn't have enough money. I told you it was one hundred and fifty rupees. Now I have nothing.' And he runs off and disappears into the Diwali shopping crowds.

Arun, who is thirty-one and works at a five-star hotel, relates how he first had sex with one of the guests, a Frenchman: 'During the six years I've been working here, I've had sex with guests only three times. I do not know how this happened with the Frenchman. I had gone to his room because he had rung for room service. I had seen him when he checked in, and he had caught my eye, but I looked away, as we are expected to. One moment, I was being formal and polite, in my role as waiter. The next minute, we were making love crazily. We were like animals. I think perhaps we looked into each other's eyes and at the same time saw the identical need there. I do not know.'

Karim tells how the first relationship he had was with a boy whom he met in a train when he was nineteen: 'He was British and travelling around India. I invited him back to our house in Lucknow. We had a big house. It was not unusual for us to have all kinds of people staying there. My parents saw it simply as their son being hospitable to a foreigner. It seemed to both of us only natural that we would have sex together, although we never spoke about it until we got into bed that first night.'

Bhirendra is twenty-eight and in the air force. His only sexual experience in his youth had been with other college boys. That stopped before he went into the service. For the next five years he did nothing, although from time to time he was aware of his attraction to the men in the barracks. He says that all the time he has been in the army, he has never seen any of his comrades naked. They always wear a dhoti at night and place a towel round their bodies while they get dressed or change their trousers. Indian men, he says, are very modest and do not like to display themselves.

'One day, in the middle of the monsoon, I don't know why, I just went into Delhi on my own. I felt this urgent need to discharge. I made up my mind that I would find someone for sex. I saw one foreigner, he was from Holland, and he was older than I am, maybe in his forties. I just followed him. He walked around Connaught Place, looked in the shops. I followed, stopped when he did. After a time, he turned round to me and said, "Why are you following me?" I didn't know what to say. I was afraid he would be angry. I just said, "I like you." He smiled and I knew it was all right. We went to a hotel and drank a beer and talked for some time. Then he took me to his hotel. We went to bed and he penetrated me. I liked it very much. I do not know where I got the courage to do such a thing.

'We became good friends. He came back to Delhi three or four times, and we took a hotel, and I took leave from the air force so we could stay together. It was very good. He was kind, and he came to meet my family close to Muzaffarnagar. They thought he was a good man. He gave us some money to buy two buffaloes. We called one Peter and the other Edward, which were his names, and my mother laughed trying to say the words. We had a very happy time.

'Then it became time for my marriage. He was angry. He told me I liked men too much to get married. I said to him I do not have the choice. I said it would make no difference to his friendship with me, but that made him even more upset. He said it was wrong. I said, "What do you want?" He said I should tell her about my friendship with him, and when I said that was not possible, he called me names. He went away, and I never heard anything more from him. I didn't understand why he would do like that. I have never found anyone else like him. I miss him. My wife and I have a baby of two years now. My wife is a good woman, and she gets on well with my mother and two sisters. I am happy. But I often think of him and wonder why he could not accept the way things are. I feel angry with him now, because I had called him brother and friend, and for me that is a very important thing. I wrote a letter to him, but he did not reply. Sometimes, I used to go Connaught Place, hoping that I might find him there, but I know that is impossible.'

This is a dramatic example of the kind of cultural disjunction between the Western concept of gay identity and the more amorphous sexuality of Indian men. A certain intransigence and an inability to accept the difference in the structure of male-to-male sexuality are the results of Western assumptions of the universal validity of their culture. That the banner of 'liberation' may also be yet another mutation of colonialism is not something that seems to have occurred to Bhirendra's friend. The discussion of gayness in India – which has only really reached the mainstream media in the past decade – is itself a product of liberalisation, of opening up to the world, and a symptom of an emerging middle class which is articulated to a consumerism that is truly international.

The relationship with the West is a recurring theme, the more so since the emerging awareness of sexual orientation, if not of sexual identity, is associated with a perception that people in the West are generally more tolerant and accepting. A number of the men spoke of wanting to leave India, because they saw the US, Europe and Australia as places where their sexual needs could more freely express themselves.

Tushar, a hotel worker, says that he has heard there is 'free sex' in the West: 'What does it mean?' he asks. He has read in a magazine that it is common for people to change partners regularly. He asks, 'How can that be? Here people have one partner for life. In India, if you do not like sex with your wife, or if she does not enjoy with you, you do it just to make children, *bas*. After you do what you can, *hath se*, you watch blue films, you go to prostitutes. Once you are married, you have to stay together because of the family.'

Rohan, a gay-identified middle-class man, says: 'I suppose what I would like most is to live with a man, but that is not possible in Delhi. I think of going abroad, because I know it is easier to live with someone of the same sex in Australia or America. Even so, I do know that the pressures of living in the West are there; they may be different, but there are still pressures. In the West, relationships do not last, people go off with someone else, it is so easy; and you can wind up as alone as you are in Delhi.'

Ibrahim, twenty-eight, former garment exporter, says: 'I had my own business, but I had so much of debt, and my creditors didn't pay. It was just at the time when I was getting married, so all that expense was also there. Before the business failed, there was one buyer who used to come from Europe, from Germany. His skin was very fair, which I liked. He was an attractive man, and I used to look forward to the times when he would come. One day, we had gone out to discuss business. We drank some beer. Afterwards we went to his hotel to continue our discussions. He gave me some whisky and we sat close together. He sucked me, and I him. This was the first time I had ever done with a man, and it was only two or three months after my marriage. Soon after that, the business was bankrupt, and he never came to Delhi again.' Ibrahim says that since the activity was initiated by the foreigner, his burden of shame is lightened: he was not even thinking of such a thing; it just happened.

Udhay, twenty, from Bihar, is working in a factory making rubber goods. He earns two thousand eight hundred rupees a month. A dark-complexioned young man, wearing burgundy-coloured trousers, shabby floral-patterned shirt and plastic chappals. His nails are ingrained with dirt from his work. He lives with his brother and sister-in-law in Chandni Chowk.

He is very much a village boy transformed into a worker. He has been sexually aware only since arriving in Delhi. At home, although they were a big family and lived in crowded conditions, he says he knew nothing of sex. He says he had never thought of why his brothers and sisters were different. He knew, of course, that animals procreate, but he had not previously associated the desires of his own body with what men and women might do together.

He wanted me to tell him about life – especially sexual life – in the West. He has seen blue films, and, in a video parlour in Chandni Chowk, he saw a film in which men were masturbating each other. He found this image disturbing. The films he has seen are all from the US and are mainly of white men and women. He admires the ease and readiness with which they make love. I explain to him that these are professionals, and that they do not represent anything like the reality of sexual experience of most people in the West. He does not want to hear that. He is also fascinated by the relationship between his brother and sister-in-law. Sometimes, he pretends to be sleeping when they are making love, and he tries to imagine what it is like. At present, he is walking through the Park, hoping to catch sight of what men are doing together. He has not yet made contact with another man; and indeed, he is not very clean, so he may have been rejected on that account. He says to me, 'What am I to do if I have sex with a man? What do you do? What does it feel like?' Until now, says Udhay, he has only done sex *hath se* (by hand) or 'sixty-two' as they call it, sixty-two being considered the number of strokes necessary to make an Indian man ejaculate – itself an ironic comment on the extreme ease with which men who are sexually continent, and therefore overeager, will climax.

Udhay is in a state of nervous stimulation, wanting sex, half afraid, unsure of his own sexual orientation. The West fascinates him, since he sees it as a place of clear sexuality, where people are uninhibited and not afraid of their own sexual needs. 'Sometimes', he says vehemently, 'I want to cut it off'; and he tugs at his cock, erect, beneath the material of his trousers. A troubled young man, disturbed in his sexuality just as his social being has been violently disrupted by the abrupt transplantation from rural to industrial life.

Noorali, twenty-three, a student of interior design, is involved in a relationship with a Westerner. I met him a number of times, and he asked me to translate into Hindi a letter from his German boyfriend, Horst. It transpires that he has met Horst only once. He was introduced to him by a friend in Calcutta. Noorali is convinced they are in love with each other. The letter is already six weeks old when, one day, I sit down on a bench with him in the Park and attempt to translate the

German's rather shaky English into my equally shaky Hindi. 'Tell me', he implores, 'not only what he says, but also what he means.'

The letter is a recognisable gay fantasy, a love letter, the tone of which does not augur well for the happy and loving future which Horst is planning for himself and his Indian friend. He asks Noorali to tell him more about himself, so that he can really get to know him and understand him. Horst says that he has had many relationships in the past, but he has found that people only want him for sex or money or whatever they can get out of him. He complains that they do not want him for himself. He thinks this may change in his relationship with Noorali. He finds the photo that Noorali sent very handsome and thinks him a truly attractive man. 'Will you really be able to understand me?' he asks. 'Can you reassure me that you will not be like the others, who have taken advantage of my kindness and generosity and have left me? I do not yet have enough money to send you for the fare from Delhi to Frankfurt, but by next summer I hope to be able to do so.'

Horst tells Noorali that two years ago he sent eight hundred Deutschmarks to a young man he had met while on holiday in Morocco. This was to have been the cost of the fare to Germany. The young man wrote to say that he was afraid to travel by air, and that he would come instead by train. Later, he wrote to say that he had no visa for France or Spain and therefore could not pass through those countries. In the end, he did not come at all. Neither did he return the money to Horst. He needed it to help his family. 'You would not do that to me?' Horst asks of his Indian friend.

Then he complains that Noorali has failed to send to him, as he requested, a sketch of his penis. 'You say it is small. What does this mean? Please send me a drawing of it. I hope you will answer all my questions, because you are a very sweet and understanding person and I love you very much.'

Noorali is as intrigued by the unconsummated relationship as his friend is. I translate as best I can. It is difficult to say anything to him, other than that he should be careful and not build up too many expectations of what may come of it.

VI

The dense weave of family, the network of kinship which controls – and sometimes smothers – people's affective lives, extends also to the working life of a majority of the men. The relentlessness of labour in India, the often exploitative hours of work, the struggle to earn enough each day to secure the nourishment that will enable them to do the same thing tomorrow: it is impossible to overstate the role of work in India.

The intensity of labour also serves to distract people from pursuing their sexual and emotional needs; as a result, pressure builds up, and the opportunity for quick release is the best many can hope for. At the same time, economic function is also a powerful component of identity. To give the impression that the men in the Park are obsessed with the pursuit of sex would be wholly false; an insight into their experience of labour needs to be set against it as a corrective, as does their commitment to family. For most, work is inescapable, a powerful discipline, often an obstacle in the path of self-expression, self-realisation or other forms of fulfilment regarded as indispensable in the West to leading a full life.

Ravi is twenty-two, from Raipur. He came to Delhi with his father, a railway worker, when he was twelve. Four years later, the father retired and left Ravi alone, working in a garment factory. The young man earns two thousand rupees a month, sharing a room with another man, for which his contribution is five hundred rupees. A thousand rupees a month is spent on food. He has to work overtime to provide other necessities, including six rupees a day for bus fares, clothes and such entertainment – an occasional Hindi movie – as is available. A pinched existence, twelve hours a day, six days a week. Sunday off is for sex. He likes the army men. Sometimes, he meets a man who will take him to his home or pay for a meal. After his father left Delhi, for six months Ravi lived in the factory where he works, on or under the benches where the sewing machines stand. There, he found his liking for men. There was one older man who used to reach in Ravi's underpants and catch his cock when he was sleeping. Staying day and night in the workplace made him ill. He had a permanent cough from the fibres of the material they worked with and the dust of the factory. Some days, he says, he went out only to find something to eat in the evening. Otherwise, it was twenty-three hours a day in one place – like a prisoner.

Balu jumped on a train in Kanpur when he was thirteen; he came to Delhi, where his brother is in the army. Balu worked in hotels, carrying glasses of tea in plastic crates for people working in offices and in the market. He became a helper on a snack stall on the road near the Jamna Masjid. He mended bicycle punctures. He became a security guard in a house in a posh colony, but was paid only four hundred rupees a month, out of which he had to pay one hundred and fifty rupees for a uniform. He had to sleep outside the house, which was often closed for months at a time when the owners were away. He slept on a mat on the upstairs terrace and was on duty twenty-four hours a day, although at night he slept. He was expected to buy all his own food. Eventually, the family employed a second guard, so that his shift was reduced to twelve hours. At that time, he was picked up by a man in a car. This man gave him a hundred rupees and also opened his eyes to the possibilities of less onerous – and far more rewarding – labour. Balu says he does not like sex with men. It is difficult work, because you always have to pretend that you are interested in them. This is not always possible. He thinks of women when he is working, and he always keeps a book of soft porn available, so that he can get himself in the mood before coming into the Park.

Suresh, who is from a Dalit family in Bihar, remembers the reality of child labour: 'I had no schooling, because the children had to help earn money. We were landless, so we had to buy many of our needs. There was only occasional work for my parents, and in any case my father drank *daru* [country liquor], as a result of which he was often unfit for work. He spent the money he earned on drink. And then work was not regular. Only at busy times in the year: when the fields were being prepared before the rain; during times of transplanting and harvesting of the rice. But for children there was always work. The landowners could employ us for a few rupees a day. No one else would run all day behind the buffaloes and goats, make sure they didn't trample the crops, wouldn't stray or be stolen, and all for ten rupees a day.

'I worked ever since I can remember, that is since I was able to understand what was expected of me in looking after the animals. Sometimes I was paid in rice, and I was always pleased, because it meant that on such days we knew we would eat properly. My parents grew gourds and vegetables around the house, which was very poor. We had two buffaloes but nowhere to keep them, so they lived with us in the hut. One died. You can't think what a tragedy that was for a poor family, because selling their milk was the only regular income my mother had. She sat with the creature, holding its head in her lap, stroking it as it died, as though she could bring it back to life. It was as if she had lost a child; worse in a way, because children do not bring in money until they are seven or eight years old.

'I remember it as a lonely time. The fields were lonely. But I had many hours where I talked to myself and kept myself company. I told myself stories. And I developed a hatred for the position my family and the other Dalit families in the village had to endure. I remember looking at the sky and listening to the wind crying in the grass; and I would see the women in the distance, their backs bent as they cut the fodder, or their loads appearing above the maize or the long grass. If I hadn't come to Delhi, I would still be there now, begging a day's work here or there, or sitting waiting for the season when the rains come.

'Here I have a job in a factory. We make chappals, cut them by machine out of big squares of rubber, drive holes in them for the crosspieces, match them and dispatch them for wrapping. It means long hours of work, sometimes twelve hours a day, but there is regular money. I get eleven hundred rupees a month, and because I sleep in the factory, I get some extra for looking after the building. So they don't have to take on any security guard. At least I have my dignity. In the villages, this you do not have. You are not free. Here, if I choose, I can leave my job and take another. It is a hard life, but it is better than where I came from. I will never go back there, except to see my family.'

Saleem is in his early forties. He also works in a garment factory, twelve hours or more daily: piecework, making garments for export, mainly to Germany, Scandinavia and Canada. He can earn up to one hundred and fifty rupees a day for garments which he knows cost thirty or forty times as much in the markets of Europe. 'People who carry them out of the country and sell them make more than we do. It is always like this – those who do the hardest labour get the least reward.

'My wife and two children came from the village to join me, but we had no place to live, and the only work for my wife was domestic work. She cannot read or write, and she found it hard to learn what her employer wanted her to do. They went back home. I can work every day of the week, but sometimes I take a Sunday to come here to enjoy.

'Life is so much pressure. There is little opportunity to relax. Workers are exploited. When we are apart from the sewing machine, we do not exist. The machine is the only thing that defines us. It is not that the factory is itself unpleasant. It is air-conditioned, but it is crowded, because they have to put sixty machines in a small space. To come here, to talk and smoke, maybe to enjoy – this makes life bearable. I send money home each month, and I will go home at *Eid*. I like to have sex with my wife, but if I could stay with one friend in the city, I would like it better. That cannot happen, so I do not even dream about it.'

Ganesh, twenty-six, from Bihar, is a rickshaw driver: 'Many men who come from Bihar do this work. All you need is enough strength in your body. It is exhausting work. People do not treat us with respect. If we go out of the roads where the rickshaws are permitted, the police will beat us or take money from us. I hire the rickshaw by the day. I pay the owner twenty-five rupees, and each day I can make fifty to sixty rupees. There are too many rickshaws in Delhi, maybe two lakhs. I live in a *jhuggi* [slum] in a camp which is behind the power station at Rajghat. There are four men, all rickshaw drivers. All the *rakh* [waste ash] from the power station settles on everything, white dust which turns to mud in the rain. I pay two hundred rupees a month for rent. Those men know nothing about sex. They never discuss such things.

'You cannot work every day, because if you do, you become worn out. In the heat, life is very hard. You become dehydrated and lose weight. Many men have TB, cough, lung problems. I sleep at nine in the night, and I am up before five in the morning.'

Not all work is as debilitating as that of the unskilled young men who must take any work they can get. For some, work is a passion.

Ramesh is twenty-eight. He comes from Aligarh in Uttar Pradesh, where his family have fifteen *bighas* of land. The land is in the middle of the rose-growing district. From here, the roses are all used in the perfume industry. Aligarh is the largest rose-growing area in the world outside of Bulgaria. Ramesh is very proud of the speciality of his region: 'These are not the roses you see for sale at the traffic lights or in little vases in the Delhi restaurants,' he says contemptuously. 'Those are not roses at all. We grow *deshi* roses, indigenous varieties, which are of very ancient origin, and they have a wonderful scent. To see the fields of roses in bloom at sunset is a wonderful sight; and the air is drenched with the smell of them.

'The work is hard. We cut the roses back in December, then they are ready to bloom in March. I go back for the harvest. We take on many village people on a casual day-labour basis. When the roses are cut, we treat them in the traditional way. They are placed in a big metal vessel, with a slow fire beneath. Then the vessel is sealed. No water must be added. The flowers are boiled like that for four hours. A liquid comes from the petals, and they simmer in that. That is the liquid we sell to the wholesale perfume manufacturers. Most of it goes to the Gulf and other countries in that region. We will make about ten thousand rupees profit per *bigha*, so much of our income comes all at the same time. This is why for the rest of the year I come to Delhi, where I work collecting debts from people who have taken loans to buy items on hire purchase – refrigerators, televisions, cars. For this I get three thousand five hundred rupees a month. I would prefer to stay at home, because I do not like this work. I am always very excited when the time of year comes when I can go home and prepare for the harvest of flowers.'

Ibrahim has had his own business but, by the age of twenty-eight, has already lost it, because his creditors failed to pay their bills. He owned a factory making garments for export. 'With a wife and two children, you cannot allow yourself to be unemployed. You must take something. Now I am working in a hotel. I'm earning only three thousand five hundred rupees a month, which is difficult, because I have known what it was to earn fifteen thousand rupees a month. It is always easy to adapt to more money, but very tough when you have to get used to less. I am working night duty at the moment, eight in the evening until eight the following morning. I would like to go abroad, but I know it is impossible these days to get a visa to go to America or Europe. I would like to start some other business, but for that you need capital, and I have no means of raising any. India is a frustrating place to live, because there is so much of corruption. And there is no honesty in other things, too. Sex is like business: the real thing happens behind the scenes, in the dark.'

Mowla Ao is a government servant in the Ministry of Agriculture. He deals with the welfare of field workers and takes his work seriously: 'Many government workers do not do their work properly. Sometimes they come only late in the morning, go for lunch, take tea and leave early. They are secure. They say that the hardest work in India is getting a job; once you have a government post, the hard work is over. I came as part of the quota for Scheduled Tribes. I am a section head, but that is not a very exalted post, and, in any case, I do not care for or believe in hierarchies. I earn seven thousand rupees a month. Two thousand goes on Provident Fund. I pay an extra thousand for enhanced pension, two thousand for rent and then the rest goes on food. I am from Nagaland, which has been neglected by the Union government. This is their compensation to us – they take clever people and give them jobs. Many Nagas want Nagaland to become independent. We are too small to survive economically. Those who get an education leave for Mumbai, Delhi, Calcutta. The people who are fighting for freedom are called insurgents by the government, just as the British government called freedom-fighters terrorists. It is a real parallel. We recognise colonialism in the northeast, because our culture is dominated by the Hindi centre. I do not like to speak Hindi, although I have to at work. Although I'm from a Scheduled Tribe – one of the most backward categories – I have no sense of inferiority. We are proud of our distinctive language and culture. People in Delhi think we must be very primitive.

'Our culture is very distinctive. There is more freedom between men and women. We used to live in harmony with the jungles and the creatures which lived there. We used to call the tigers "elder brother", because like that, people thought they would not attack them. Of course the tigers have largely gone now.

'We belong to various clans within the tribe. It was forbidden to marry anyone from within the same clan. People believed that if you did so, the tigers would know. They could smell it somehow, and they would attack such people. If a young man and a young woman from the same clan were going off into the jungle together, people still say, jokingly, "Be careful, or the tigers will get you." We were animists until converted to Christianity by the British. My mother died a Catholic, but my father was an animist to the end of his life.

'We get government jobs under the reservations system. That is supposed to give advantage to those who are "backward". I do not believe there is anything backward about our culture. It was noble and lived in harmony with our surroundings. We did not damage the environment.'

The system of reservations causes great resentment among young people from the upper castes, who believe that, despite their superior qualifications, their opportunities have been limited because of the number of places set aside for the socially disadvantaged. Jairam, twenty, is from Northern Uttar Pradesh. He was due to enter medical college but failed the interview because his English was not up to the required standard.

'I do not know if I will have a chance, because now there are reservations for all these people from lower castes, who have no ability; and however good I am, I cannot take their seats. It is not fair. If people cannot come up through merit, they should not come up at all. This is especially true in the medical profession. What is the good of reserving places for people to become doctors, if they do not have the skills and ability which the work requires? It has made me very angry. I am a Rajput, even though my father is not rich, a small farmer only. Many Scheduled Caste people who will get seats in medical college will know even less English than I do, but because for them the standard is lower, they will not be refused. I think this will cause a revolution in India; so many people from the higher castes are seeing that their children are refused opportunity because the places must be given to those inferior to them in achievement. They will not tolerate it. When the Mandal Commission recommendations were put into practice by the V. P. Singh government, there were riots in UP. Many people were killed.'

Jairam is open about his desire to become a doctor. 'I want to make money, and this is a good way to do it. There is one doctor living close to our place at R. K. Puram, who has built a big house and has a smooth life. Delhi is a place where there is a lot of sickness, so being a doctor will always give you employment. You know, the air of Delhi is bad, the water is not clean. There are many children with diarrhoea, breathing disorders, asthma. There are many mosquitoes which can spread malaria. Delhi makes people ill. Making them better is a good job. It also helps them.'

A number of men who have sex with men work in hotels. Some stated explicitly that this work attracted them because a hotel is one of the few places where you can meet people who are passing through: 'You can go into their bedrooms. If they are alone, sometimes you may get to enjoy with them.'

Tushar, housekeeper in a four-star hotel, said, 'Sometimes a guest will call room service, but you are not quite sure what they want. There was an American, he called me to take some laundry. He took off his underpants while I was standing there. I looked away, but I knew that he wanted to show himself to me.'

Arun is thirty-one, of Nepalese origin. He was born in Meghalaya and speaks a sweet professional English. He works in one of Delhi's biggest hotels: 'I am chief steward in food and beverages. There is a chance that I may become captain, because the new manager in f and b is also a hill man, and he has taken a liking to me. Maybe this is because we are the only two with Chinky features.

'Two of my sisters are teachers. This was the work I first did when I finished my studies. But I had no authority over a room full of four and five year olds. I knew this was not what I wanted to do. I had a friend who knew someone in Delhi. I had written to this man; then, one day, I just took off by train, like that. An impulse. A journey of three days. I just went to his room and knocked on the door, because I had no other contact in Delhi. He didn't know me, and he was not particularly pleased to see me, but we later became good friends.

'He knew someone working at the hotel, although his position was not very high, a shoe polisher or something. One day he told me some interviews were taking place. He said I should just turn up with my biodata for interview. I joined the line waiting outside the f and b department, and I was accepted because of my English. The English is not really to my credit, but to that of my teacher, who told me to listen to the BBC. So I have the BBC to thank for my job!

'While I'm serving people, I know how to be polite – a little distant, respectful, yes, yet at the same time warm and welcoming. That is professionalism. People like it. Sometimes, if it is not too busy, I will stop and talk to them. I am at present waiting in the Italian restaurant in the hotel. The manager recently received a four-page letter from an American praising my efficiency and willingness to please.

'I am not servile, even though I accept it is my job to serve. How do I feel about the customers? Indifference. Perhaps that is not quite the right word. But neutral. They come for one or two days, and then they go; I will never see them again. I remain, I have to, that is my job. What else can I feel? I do not envy them. I know their lives and mine are far apart.

'The hotel is theatre. They see the façade, and I'm part of it. They pay for that. But we know what goes on out of their sight. I do not feel I am working below my capacity. Sometimes it is difficult to keep up with all the people you have to please, so you are trying to make yourself agreeable to ten people at once. It is exhausting, but satisfying.

'I earn only two thousand two hundred rupees a month. That is very little. With tips, it will come to four to five thousand rupees. Never in my wildest dreams did I ever think I would come so far. So I am absolutely satisfied.

'Sometimes sex has happened with guests. Rarely. For most of the time, at work I do not think about it. Sometimes it comes close. You think it could happen. But it is for them to take the initiative. I'm only an employee. But then, occasionally, carnal instincts take over.

'In the hotel, the people who get on are apple polishers – that is, those who stick to the rules, who don't ask questions. The *chamchas* [yes-men]. I know if I want to be successful, I must be more than good at my job. Being gay also drives you; you want to be as good as, if not better than, everybody else.'

99

There is no doubt that the growth in the hotel, business, travel and tourist industries in India also spreads forms of consciousness which permit and facilitate the expression of same-sex attraction. The difference is striking between those working in sweated industries and those who have entered the more open-minded world of catering and service which involves international travellers.

Some of the most intense work discipline naturally occurs in the armed services, and many servicemen are to be found from time to time in the Park. Their lives are highly controlled, regulated and timetabled. Some like this structuring of their lives, even though many older men find it irksome.

Raju is a young army recruit from near Merut. He is accompanied by an officer, a very smart man of about forty, whose tin box Raju carries on his head. The officer goes off to talk with some *khotis* who are gathered under a neem tree close to the lake. While Raju watches, he negotiates with them and then disappears into the jungle with one boy. The young soldier waits patiently on a bench and places the tin box beside him. In full dark-green uniform, his skin is very dark, his eyes vivid white, the pupils a light hazel. He has one brother in the army, two other brothers and four sisters. The family has forty *bighas* of land. They buy nothing in the market but salt, sugar and clothes. They grow rice, maize, wheat, vegetables, *urad* [a pulse], beans.

He likes army life, having been in Delhi for less than a year. He does not mind getting up at 4.30 a.m., for this is the practice at home. 'We wash and use the latrine, then do physical training. After that, there is breakfast, chapatis and milk. Then arms practice. More exercise before lunch of vegetables, dal and chapatis. We sleep early in the afternoon, then more physical training. After a shower, there is one hour of free time, when we read, play cards, talk. Then supper of rice, vegetables and dal. Lights out by nine-thirty. I like it. It is regular, secure, predictable. You know what is going to happen each day.'

Amit, thirty-two, is an army mechanic. His wife and child live not far away, in Ghaziabad. He has been in the army for ten years. Just before Diwali, he says he will be on duty over the festival period. He has to be available in case any vehicle breaks down when the top brass are moving from place to place, even though, at this time of year, they may simply be going from party to party. Amit is paid four thousand rupees a month.

Amit's family have ten *bighas* of land. As well as his wife and child, he has three sisters who depend on him. A serious man, very smartly dressed, today he is carrying a folder of documents, since he is on his way to a private school to register the children of his commanding officer for next term. Such errands are not officially part of his job, but it would be unthinkable to refuse, since his life in the army is not arduous. Only the long hours of being available are irksome. When the vehicles have to be mended, he enjoys it.

He will stay in the army for the seventeen years necessary to secure a pension; then he will take some other job. Amit goes home less often than he should. Instead of returning to his family on Sundays, he often comes to the Park. He likes older men. The proximity of the camp to this place is one of the best things about the job. He finds the strict timetable very tiresome; but there are always ways of finding a way out. In any case, his commanding officer had sex with him for some years, so if he should get into trouble, there is always someone who will help him out.

Ram Singh, after fifteen years in the air force, also chafes at the severity of the discipline. 'I am in the non-technical sector, based in Shillong in Meghalaya. Earlier, I was in Bangalore. Now that I am married, I live in married quarters, which gives me some privacy in camp, even though, of course, my wife remains at home. The bachelors all sleep in one room – thirty beds. There is absolutely no privacy. But Indian men are very modest in public. You never see each other without clothes. The men get used to going without sex. Masturbation is the maximum. You never see a hard cock. Being in the air force, you cannot do anything with another man on pain of social shame and instant dismissal from the service.

'I've now completed fifteen years in the air force. You get a pension now only after twenty years. It used to be after fifteen; so I'll have to stay another five, before I get a job outside. I'm not very business minded, I don't know what I'll do. According to air force rules, I'm not even supposed to talk to a foreigner. I cannot have a friendship with a foreigner, even though I have no secrets, I pose no threat to the security of India.

'I learned English in the air force and through my relationship with the man from Ireland. Life in the air force is tedious. The rules remain from British times – like so many others: make them work hard, get up at five, sleep at nine-thirty; exercises, activity, games that will take their minds off other things, so that they will not think of emotional deprivation or sexual frustration. I earn three thousand five hundred rupees a month, and when I retire, I'll get a pension of one thousand five hundred rupees.'

Dhirendra is in his mid thirties. From Haryana, he joined the army when he was eighteen. He is one of seven brothers who, between them, have thirty *bighas* of land. He looks forward to the time when he can leave the army, with a pension of one thousand five hundred rupees a month and, he hopes, a gratuity of two or three lakhs of rupees With this, he will go back to his village and start a business, maybe a shop, he doesn't yet know. He saw active service in Sri Lanka, when the Indian Peacekeeping Force went in. He saw many deaths at that time.

He is now bored with army life: 'When you are young, it is exciting. You move away from home and find experiences you cannot have in the village. But when you have been from one barracks to another, they all look the same. The routine is very boring. You get up at four-thirty, shower, exercise, breakfast, arms practice, lunch, rest, more exercise, supper, sleep. Every day is the same. But when you go on active service, it is different, but not in a way that is pleasant. You see your friends killed, you kill others. The routine is very strict. It keeps your body and mind occupied.

'I was married and have one son. My wife died of cancer four years ago. I come here for sex, but I am looking for friends, for comfort. The army is a cold place.'

Vajpal has been in the army for sixteen years. He has three children: a boy of seventeen, a girl of twelve and a boy of seven. The family lives in Delhi, in Chanakyapuri; but Vajpal stays in barracks and goes home only from time to time. 'Like that, I have the best of both worlds. I prefer the world of men. Not just because I like sex with men; I am fifty-fifty. It is the same thing to me, if I fuck a man or a woman, it is the person who counts. But men's interests and women's interests are different and they cannot be reconciled. I am a lover of all kinds of sport. I have been a wrestler, a boxer, I was in the all-army team. I love cricket and athletics. I like football. Now I am coaching young people in the army. Athletes and sportsmen have a privileged life in the army. I have now the rank of captain. I earn seven thousand rupees a month.

'I love my family, but I do not wish to be with them all the time. The army teaches people how to behave. The discipline becomes second nature. Up at four, regular meals, even shit to a timetable. But we are taught about sex. We know it is necessary to wear a condom for sex; we have instruction on personal hygiene. With my wife, I do not use a condom, but with anyone else, I always carry, so that way, I will not take any bad thing back home.'

Vajpal suggests the power of the sexual apartheid that exists in India, and which is institutionalised in the armed services: 'the world of men and the world of women exist side by side; but their interests are mutually exclusive. They come together only for the purposes of the family, the creation of human networks of security and continuity. Apart from that, they have their own lives.'

Vajpal sits with a twenty-year-old Nepalese boy, stunningly beautiful, who lies with his head in the older man's lap. This boy is a sex worker. He has no other occupation, but can command a good price. In any case, he is devoted to this fellow. The boy says he too is fifty-fifty. He says he first had sex at the age of twelve or thirteen, and with a girl when he was sixteen. He came to India with his family as a child. He lives with his brother and uncle. He thinks about the future, but having left school after the Fourth Standard, he has no qualifications for any other work. Sex work is not a career. It is part-time, casual. Not a job for life.

A man of about forty says he is a Black Cap Commando, one of the elite of the corps of bodyguards of VIPs. He says he has been assigned to the protection of various Congress leaders, including Rajesh Pilot. He boasts of the celebrities he has known and says he loves this life, which is a 'real man's life'. He tells how one soldier in the guard was killed defending a senior Congress politician.

'I had to inform his wife. When I reached the home, I found she was four months pregnant. She was staying with her mother-in-law. They asked me to stay with them in the house for a couple of days. I was in the bathroom, and this woman came in when I had no clothes on. She wanted me to make love to her. I said, "Impossible. You are pregnant with your dead husband's child." Nothing happened between us. Later, I came to know she had committed suicide.'

The police, especially those who live in barracks, also lead a life of considerable discipline. Pradeep, thirty-eight, stays in the police compound of the Central Reserve Police Force. 'I like the company of men. I prefer it to domestic life. I enjoy going home, of course, but I like the excitement of my work. We do duty in Tihar Jail sometimes, and then we are sent to various places all over the country if there is some need, when there is trouble – a bomb outrage, atrocities against lower-caste people, some social unrest. I will never be able to go home and settle into my village after the life I have known. I will open some business where I still have the chance to roam around.

'Sometimes the police come into the Park to raid it. They only want some excitement, maybe some fun, you know, sex, or to get some money. They will have sex with the *khotis*, then afterwards take some money from them as well. Of course, I do not tell the men I work with that I too am like that. They will not admit in private that they also enjoy. But when there is a group of them, they may take some boys from the Park, arrest them, then have sex with them. They will pretend they do it only because they despise them, but they really want to enjoy also. If they arrest them, they will get free sex and at the same time say they are doing their duty. This is very convenient. I do not blame them. Who will not abuse the power he has, if he has the opportunity?'

The vast unemployment of India is also represented in the Park: not only the graduates without work, but the young men from the villages without qualifications and those who work in the sex trade. A few make a tolerable living out of this, but many more work only casually, to supplement an income, to combine some gain with pleasure. Those who take it seriously are always on the lookout, making sure they are conspicuous to all the men who pass by.

Tariq is twenty-one, slim, wide smile, high – and already receding – hairline, pale. He wears tight clothes that show off his elegant figure. He comes from Calcutta and lives with his sister and her family in Transyamuna. His only work is in the parks, where he will suck for twenty or thirty rupees. He admits that the price is arbitrary, because he cannot compel people to pay. Like many of the *khotis*, his self-esteem is low. He does not think he is good-looking, says his skin is black. Some days he will get one or two customers, others as many as five or six. He does not penetrate or allow himself to be penetrated.

He meets his friends here. Little knots of *khotis* form and dissolve all the time, as they negotiate with a *giriya* or walk off together. They are always saying they are leaving, because the day is *khali* (empty); they go as far as the tea-stall and then return. Tariq comes three or four times a week to the Park. He also visits the area around Old Delhi railway station, New Delhi station, the Plaza bus stand, Nehru Park on Sundays. His life is structured around sexual cruising and being available at the moment when other people's needs are at their most insistent. 'Being there at the right moment': it is a highly skilled, opportunistic but precarious job.

Shankar is now twenty-seven. I met him for the first time five years ago at India Gate: at that time, he had just arrived in Delhi, eager for any contact, hungry to explore same-sex relationships. He is from Mangalore, where his family grow coconuts, cashews and paddy. They grow 1500 quintals of rice for the market and keep as much again for their annual consumption. There are three brothers and three sisters. When the land has been subdivided there will be little for each of them.

Shankar is a thin man with dark skin, a long thin face. When I first met him, he said he was desperate for sex and spent most of his time looking for it. He took severe risks: he knew short-time hotels and quiet corners in Delhi, such as the extreme-side seats in some of the movie houses, from where you are almost invisible to the rest of the people in the audience. It is a piquant situation – one of the most crowded places in the city can also provide cover for sexual activity. He has friends who occasionally let him use their rooms. He has never really bothered about getting a proper job but has worked as a waiter in a number of cafés and restaurants in Delhi.

He has known he liked men since he was fourteen; but it took him another ten years to realise that men also may like him, and that there is money to be earned from it. He has just finished a three-month contract working in the canteen of the Punjabi National Bank. He has now been retrenched but may get another three-month contract. But the primary preoccupation of his life in Delhi has been the pursuit of sex.

When I met him in March 1997, he was cruising a bus stand. He stopped me and asked if I remembered him. I did and, indeed, recalled his name, although he had forgotten mine. He has become more thoughtful in the three years since I last saw him. He says he now regrets having neglected his career for the sake of instant sex and instant money. He has had no long-term relationship and has known a terrible loneliness, saying that 'conditions in Delhi are not favourable for repeated meetings. Sexual release is all that people want. This is easy. It is everywhere – in the buses, at the bus stands, in the toilets, in the parks. Even in the streets, you can pick people up. You recognise it in eyes that search the faces of strangers looking for the same thing.'

Shankar is now living with his brother, who came to Delhi last year and now works in a hotel. Shankar himself is on the margin of a casual labour market; at twenty-seven, he is too old for those who are willing to pay for sex. 'One day, a boy who is working as a professional came to me and said, "What are you doing?" I told him I was working in the canteen at the bank. "Why don't you ask around there and see if you can get me some customers? There must be many among all those men. I'll give you twenty per cent for each one you get me." I couldn't do that. I wouldn't want anyone in the place where I work to know I am like that.'

Shankar is drifting. His English is good, from school and from many casual contacts. It is too late for him to repair an education disrupted by his pursuit of sex. One day he will go home to be married, 'if I do not find a foreigner or someone to take care of me'. He asks me about the chance of work in Europe. I tell him of the problem with visas, the restrictions Europe is placing on people from outside. He does not believe me. He thinks I am just saying this to discourage him, because I do not want him in my country.

He knows of one man who paid Rs 350,000 to go abroad and is now in the US. Many boys pay agents and middlemen, who then disappear with the money. He knew of the ship that sank on Christmas Day 1996, with its fateful cargo of doomed migrants. He says he feels like a migrant without a destination: he cannot return to Mangalore; Delhi is not his home. He says, 'There is nowhere for men like me in India. I want to go out. But every exit is blocked.'

There is one more indicator that reveals something of the wider circumstances of these men's lives: the nature of the household they live in. I asked each of them who they were living with:

Extended family (parents, wife and children):	3
Joint family (parents, siblings and their families):	5
Nuclear family (wife and children):	12
With parents:	7
Alone:	5
Shared lodgings:	13
Hostel:	2
In the workplace:	3
In army or police barracks:	9
With other relatives (brother, cousins, etc.):	9
With friends:	1
Homeless:	2
With another man in a sexual relationship:	1
Wouldn't say/Unknown:	3

The living arrangements of the men reflect patterns of migration: relatively few live in joint or extended families. The nuclear family is common. The large number of men in lodgings – all with other men, be they workmates or colleagues – suggests both the reluctance of men to live alone and the expense of doing so. Again, it shows the close network of relationships in which most men live, and the difficulty they face in their search for unconventional sexual outlets. It also reflects the ambiguities of 'community', the support and strength it offers, but also its controlling, policing aspect.

VII

The apartness of the sexual experience of men with men suggests that it is accommodated only reluctantly into the impermeable networks of family and kin in India; it exists elsewhere than in the arena of real life. Many men look upon Delhi as the only place in which such activity is thinkable. The city becomes the site where traditional relationships can be modified, where extraordinary things can happen and where greater freedoms may be achieved; the other face of this is that Delhi is the site of temptation, where the innocent may be corrupted and the guileless seduced. It is also a place of disorientation and confusion. Above all, it is where secrets can be kept, which is not the case in the village or the small country town.

'When I first came to Delhi,' says Nataranjan from Orissa, 'I lived with my auntie in Noida. They are good people, but they would always wait for me until I came home, and I had to hurry to get there in time for meals at eight in the evening. Family members in India feel they have the right to know what you have been doing, where you have come from, who you have been seeing. They do so out of affection and a sense of responsibility, but I had come to Delhi for something else. So I shifted to Ghaziabad, where I have a place alone. It is a two-roomed apartment which is far cheaper than anything similar would be in Delhi itself. I have a kind of freedom that few people in Delhi can know. I can listen to music whenever I choose, watch TV, turn on the video whenever I wish. I can also take friends there, which is the most important thing, for there is no one to ask questions about the nature of my relationship with them. . . . My parents are Oriya. They will have no wish to come to Delhi. There are things in my life which it is best for them not to know, and since I am to be married next year, things that my wife certainly must not come to know.'

Mahesh, twenty, one of the professionals in the Park, says: 'I came to Delhi from Bihar to join my brother, who pedals a cycle-rickshaw. I wanted something, but I didn't know what it was. I soon found out in Delhi that I wanted sex. It didn't take long to discover Central Park and this place. When I found out I could also get men to pay me, I stopped doing the rough, casual jobs I had had before. . . . The things I do here do not happen at home. I now know what was drawing me to come here. Delhi is a teacher. I learned more through Delhi than I did in all my time at school.'

Harish, a twenty-year-old gay-identified man, came from Bhopal to

Delhi to study: 'I knew when I came to Delhi two years ago that I was gay. There are so many people in Delhi, you find contacts very quickly. The crowds are so great that you can hide in them. You learn to find people who are like you by a look, a glance, a movement of the face. No one knows what is going on, and that gives you anonymity. It makes it more secure.'

Pandu, twenty-seven, from Karnataka, left his village at seventeen to come to Delhi: 'We have some land near Hubli, but I wanted a job. I found it easy to get work, as a room boy in a guesthouse in south Delhi. There I met one man, an Indian who had come back from the US, who became my great friend. He asked me into his room one night, and we had sex. For eighteen months he looked after me; and it is thanks to him that I am now successful, with a proper job.

'When I first came to the city, I did not know anything. I didn't know which places to go to to find what I wanted. After some time, I learned that Nehru Park is a meeting place. The first time I went there, I met a man who was staying in a hotel. I was very frightened, but I went with him, and it was fine. Now I know everything. I am familiar with every place. I know the bus stands and the toilets, the parks and the markets. I always get on buses that are crowded because sometimes you can find people that way.

'I also have a wife and two children in the village, although nobody here knows it. It is a secret. Delhi is like that: it will not betray our secrets, it can be kind to you. If you want to hide, Delhi will conceal you. I like to keep the two parts of my life separate, so they do not come into contact in any way. In Delhi I am a gay man, but when I go home, people see me as the successful village boy who went to the great city to find work and has made a success of his life.'

Yusuf, now eighteen, and also a professional in the Park, came to Delhi from Patna in Bihar when he was twelve: 'My first experience was in Central Park, when I was fourteen. A man, who must have been in his middle twenties, took me behind some bushes. He didn't penetrate me, but put his cock between my thighs. I always knew that I wanted this, and I have made a life out of it since that time. I have no wish to do any other work. I like the days in the Park. I meet my friends, I enjoy, I get money. You never know what each day is going to bring. One day, I may meet someone who is well off, who will rescue me, take me to live in an apartment or a hotel, or go abroad with me. I cannot now go back to the village. I have four brothers and three sisters there. There is no homosex in the village. You have to come to Delhi for this; this is my life, and I cannot do anything else. I do not want to.'

Mowla Ao from Nagaland also found Delhi his chief instructor in the exploration of his sexuality: 'I had no experience with men until I came to Delhi, although I had had sex with a woman at home. I later found out that she used to seduce many college boys. I discovered the Park only last year, although I have been in Delhi for five years. I used to go to a public toilet at the end of the bus route close to where I stay, where men used to go late in the night for sex. I found that by accident. I like to go there to watch sometimes. Since I found the Park, I have become an addict. I come every Saturday and Sunday, almost every week, and when there is a holiday from work. Whenever I feel lonely, I come here. I have met some good people. Many men from the army. They are usually clean and have discipline and they are honest. Mostly they have a condom with them. I like that. A man with a good body. I do not like fat people. It is a long way to have come from Nagaland. When I was there, I was very innocent. The pleasures of young people are very simple. We laugh and take pleasure in small things – going on a picnic, teasing one another. I feel sad that such activities no longer delight me. I have been spoiled by Delhi; although I like it here and would not wish to go back to the northeast, I think I have also lost a part of myself in the journey from there to here.'

A number of the men I met were about to go home, to the village, to the family. Some were going on leave, for a festival or just for a vacation to see their families. Two or three said explicitly that they had come to the Park to have sex with a man in order to help them when they had sex with their wives: the stimulus, the memory of the encounter would excite them, so that they could do what was expected of them when they reached home. This also reinforced the impression of Delhi as a place where anything can happen, from which the village environment, the place where all that is honourable and dutiful is located, must be preserved. A kind of purification ritual in a place polluted not by caste contact, but by the even more mysterious and troubling contaminant of an unavowable sexuality.

It is just before Diwali. There is greater activity than usual in the Park. Samir is going home to his village close to Aligarh. He is a security guard, working nights in a Japanese-owned factory in Gurgao. Before going home, he wants to have sex with a man, because this will help him with his conjugal duties tomorrow. He says this quite openly: 'I will remember the looks, the touch, the smell of men before I can make love to my wife. This will excite me, but without it, I will have great difficulty.' Samir is twenty-eight, very smart, with an almost military bearing and close-cropped hair. He has one child, a girl of three. He likes women, but does not enjoy sex with them.

An air force man is just going home on leave for fifteen days. Before he goes, he is visiting the Park. He carries a small bag containing his clean clothes, his walkman and tapes that will keep him entertained when he gets to his village. It is only a three-hour bus journey away. He has a wife and two children in Haryana, but has come to enjoy before going. 'If I have sex with a man, it makes it easier. I prefer to have sex with a man. This helps me to do my duty to my wife. If I find someone who has a place, I will stay with him tonight and go home tomorrow. I've been in the air force for ten years. Camp is sexless. You have to come out here to enjoy. If I find a man today and can spend the night, I will take his cock into my mouth, suck his balls, feel his cock inside me. That will satisfy me for two weeks. No one can see what is going on inside your head. My wife will never know what I do here.'

A more disturbing experience is a touching encounter with a young Adivasi (tribal) in the Park. I am sitting on a concrete bench overlooking the glassy stagnant water of one of the ponds. It is a warm day in March. The wind is blowing the dead leaves from the trees, and the waxy red bells of cottonsilk flowers fall with a faint thud into the dust. Over the water dragonflies iridescent in the sunshine; an occasional flash of blue of a kingfisher. I am talking to a man who is visiting Delhi on business from the private hospital in Andhra Pradesh where he is a medical orderly. He was formerly in the army, posted in Delhi. He is married with two children. Today, he is visiting the scene where he had much sexual enjoyment ten years ago.

As we talk, I am aware of a presence hovering on the edge of our conversation; and then a slight figure sits cautiously on the edge of the bench. At first I ignore him, thinking it simply someone else who wants to listen to what a foreigner has to say. When the older man gets up to go, this young man smiles at me.

He is nineteen, and from Raigad, one of the poorest parts of Madhya Pradesh. His name, he says, is James, and he is a Christian, converted like many of the tribal people in that area at the end of the nineteenth century. He is pitifully thin. He wears a faded shirt, shabby trousers and the cheapest plastic chappals. His feet are scarred and rough, as though unused to shoes. He is not very clean. His skin is dark, his smile regular and transforming, his teeth shine like silver. Although he has an English name, he speaks little English.

He has been in Delhi only a few months. He lives with his brother, his brother's wife and their three children in two rooms at Palam colony, near the international airport. The brother has a menial and low-paid government job at the airport, under the quota reserved for the Scheduled Tribes.

James shares a room with the three children. He worked in a factory when he first arrived in Delhi, but – unused to the discipline of industry – he soon became unemployed. He is a weak young man, frail and vulnerable, and he has been taken advantage of, sexually, by many

113

men who come to the Park. He has a kind of wistful grace and youthful pliability which make him obviously attractive to men. Having no work, he has accepted ten or twenty rupees, derisory sums, from them, often nothing at all. He lacks confidence and seems ashamed of being an Adivasi, ashamed of being an ill-instructed man from a 'backward' area, ashamed of being illiterate, ashamed of his dark skin.

It is difficult to talk to him about what has happened to him. He has clearly found this place and knows what happens here (how?). He is trying to earn some money to pay his brother, since the brother brought him to Delhi to work and to help out with the family, as well as to send something back to Raigad. One brother and sister remain there with his mother. His father died when he was small. There are two other brothers, both in the army. As he speaks of Raigad, his face changes, his voice becomes stronger and his eyes shine. Where they live, it is still jungle. He knows where to find herbs for medicine against fever, diarrhoea and headaches; he understands which roots and wild fruits will supplement their diet. He can make rope from creepers and catch fish in the streams with his bare hands. The houses are of wood and earth, the floors and walls strengthened with cow dung to harden them. He helped rebuild the house in which the family live, and he knows how to make thatch so that it will resist the monsoon. He is utterly astonished at the questions I ask about his home, which suggest to him that I recognise the beauty of his environment and his sense of loss and bewilderment at being displaced in the city.

The Adivasis are the oldest inhabitants of India. Are you not proud of belonging to them? I ask. But we are poor, he says. How can you be poor, I say, since your people have lived for thousands of years and have survived, while so many conquerors of India have come and gone? He tells how his people still talk of the Marathas, who came to raid the tribal people, took their cattle and land and tried to chase them from the jungle. Then the British came and gave them Christianity, although they also made them trespassers in their own forests.

In Delhi, this young man is confused and ill at ease. Delhi has made him shabby and poor, when in his home he would be proud and confident. I offer him fifty rupees. He refuses and turns away in shame and embarrassment. Now it is my turn to be embarrassed. He believes that being black is a stigma; he does not like his beautiful black skin. He remains a victim of a long and consistent inferiorisation of those who have sustained India for millennia, and whose non-violent way of life is a reproach and bitter counterpoint to contemporary forms of development.

We sit and buy some tea close to the entrance to the Park, on rocks that stink of piss, in the shadow of a crimson bougainvillaea. James's native tongue is not even known in Delhi. He gets up at four in the morning, because that has always been his custom; and he goes to sleep at nine. He tells me that he does not like the Park, but he has been coming daily for several weeks.

I see him several times in the following weeks and develop a sweet friendship with him. He sometimes sits next to me and takes my hand, and when I leave the Park, he comes with me to the bus stand and waves to me as the bus moves away. Shortly before I leave Delhi, I ask him what he would like me to bring when I return from England after a few weeks. I expect he will say a walkman or a watch or a pair of Nike trainers. Instead, he says, 'A rosary'. In London I buy a pretty rosary at Westminster Cathedral, but when I get back to Delhi, he has gone. He no longer comes to the Park. 'What happened?' I ask. No one knows. Maybe the men grew tired of him and didn't give him money, so he stopped coming. In the end, I gave the rosary to another friend, also a tribal and a Christian.

A few months later, I see him again. He had been back to Raigad, but there the lack of occupation had driven him once more to Delhi. He had found work as a security guard; but he was required to work two shifts, fourteen hours in all, and he had given it up after two or three days. In a plastic bag he is carrying the uniform, the military-looking cap and jacket, which he is returning to the company. He said, 'I do not like such work.' It is the voice of the countryman resisting the transformation from the rhythm of the seasons to the altered tempo of industrial life. I want to say to him, 'This is the way it is. That is what the city means.' He says he will not stay, oscillating between home and the city, torn between the consolations of the metropolis and the comforting predictability of home.

Delhi, then, is, in reality as well as in fantasy, a place of danger and exploitation, as well as of expanding horizons and hopeful opportunity.

Rahul tells how Delhi was responsible for the bad company he fell into in his teens: 'I went with my boyfriend when I was seventeen to the Maurya Sheraton with an old Englishman, who had met us in Connaught Place. My friend stole his wallet, and we went on a spending spree, buying clothes, a camera, records, a watch. It is very easy to take advantage of such people, because they are afraid of the police, and they will not want to admit in public that they have invited boys who are only seventeen to their hotel room.'

Karam, twenty-three, and his friend, Dilip, who is only fifteen, are playing a profitable game around Central Park. Karam is from near Agra, and his friend is from Old Delhi. Karam picks up men who seem well-to-do or who are foreign in Connaught Place. He tells them he is gay and wants to have sex with them. He says he is working in a travel agency off Connaught Place and has the key, so it will be perfectly safe. Dilip is actually working as security guard for the travel agency. Once they get the man in the office, Karam offers him Dilip as a sexual partner. The door is locked, and the man finds himself captive; unless he parts with all his money and valuables, they threaten to tell the police that he has made advances to a young boy. This is usually enough to make him give them what they want.

They are completely open about what they do. Karam says he has no work, and Dilip earns only a few hundred rupees a month at his job. He says that he has to contribute to the family income. They are quite unconcerned with the morality of their version of small-time extortion and prostitution. Karam's father is dead, and his family without resources. 'No problem,' he says; 'you can't live without money, so it is up to you to get it. If you can't earn it, you must make it. If you can't make, you must take.' No, he knew nothing of sex before coming to Delhi; he was picked up one day by a man who took him to a hotel, and that is what gave him the idea.

It is a familiar story, that sex with men is not possible in the rural areas and the small towns from which many of the men come. In fact, of the non-Delhi born, as many as thirteen out of fifty-five (about 23 per cent) said that they did not believe it happened in their home place. One man said he knew 'for sure' that such things were unknown in Chennai; another that in Bhopal it was impossible. This is part of a construction that wants to separate 'home', a place of childhood and primal innocence, from the depravity of the city. At times, it is also obliquely an expression of resentment at the social and economic forces that disturbed their lives, that compelled them to leave home, that sent them away in search of livelihood. This is a counterweight to the idea that the city is a place of excitement, unpredictability, new and uncharted relationships and possibly even wealth.

But even those who live, work and have been brought up in the city do not always see it like this. Some of these men have a different kind of rationalisation for their sexual activity with other men, and many fall back on the idea that but for the scarcity of women, they would never dream of doing any such thing. Perhaps the most illuminating story was that of two security guards, Anup and Shantaram, who both guard houses in a posh suburb of Delhi.

Anup is from Eastern Uttar Pradesh and Shantaram from near Dehra Dun. They are friends and know each other from sitting in adjacent sentry boxes outside neighbouring houses in Green Park. Anup is twenty-six and Shantaram twenty-eight; both are unmarried. Anup used to work in a factory; Shantaram was a driver but was hurt in an accident that almost killed his employer. Since then he has worked as a guard. They do long hours. At night, they sit, muffled in Balaclavas and shawls against the cold. In summer, they have to turn their boxes away from the suffocating glare of sunlight. They spend their time sitting, watching who comes and goes, reading newspapers and paperback Hindi novels. Sometimes they play cards when the owners of the houses are away. They have plenty of time to reflect on life and to philosophise on wealth and poverty, fate, caste, corruption, the lives of the rich and the lives of their own poor families.

Their conversation often turns to sex. Both have had sex with other men, although this in no way disturbs their sense of being male. Anup, by way of explaining the flexibility of his sexual preferences, says, 'Sometimes, anything is better than nothing. But not always. It depends.' He tells how, once when he was standing in a crowded bus travelling through Uttar Pradesh on his way home, a man placed his hand over his genitals. 'I slapped him. The man started to shout and he accused me of hitting him for no reason. The driver stopped the bus. I told everybody in the bus that I had slapped him because he had tried to assault me indecently. Everyone on the bus got very angry with this man and started to beat him. He had to get out of the bus, and he was left standing in the road a long way from his destination.' Then, on another occasion, Anup says, he fucked a man he met on the Delhi buses. This man had done the same thing, but this time Anup didn't protest. He says, 'We got down from the bus near Delhi Ridge, and we went into the forest. I did it at that time because I was feeling need. Sometimes you feel you want to and sometimes you don't. It depends on how great your need is. Sometimes you have to empty what is in your balls.'

'You need discharge,' explains Shantaram, who has been listening and nodding to his friend's account of his experience; he says he feels the same. 'Sometimes you feel you want some release. If there is no woman, then a man will sometimes do. If he is young it is better, but it doesn't really matter if you have the feeling. I have done it even with a man of forty. But if you do not feel like it, you refuse.' 'But why,' I

asked Anup, 'do you strike a man in the bus like that, when you sometimes like to enjoy with men?' He says, 'I do not like to enjoy with
men. Sometimes I do it, but only when there is no alternative. It is
better', he says wisely, 'to have someone than no one. But it is not
always better to have anyone rather than no one.'

I asked the two security men if they would ever behave like that
in their villages. Of course not, they said. We are with our families
there. If you were to do such a thing, you would be punished. You
would never find a wife. Both say that they will get married 'next year'
– a response that came up no fewer than eight times with the interviewees. It is clear that 'next year' is also a metaphor for 'sometime',
perhaps in the not too distant future.

But of course sex does happen in the villages: in the men's accounts
of their introductions to sex, a significant minority of migrants had their
first experience close to home – fourteen out of fifty-five, or 25 per
cent. Some of their stories hint at the kind of things that do indeed
occur in the villages, as they do everywhere; and the fact that they are
mostly concealed and secret, and that to disclose them would be dangerous, is true not only of Delhi but also of many other places in the world,
particularly when these incidents involve children and close family
members.

Anand is thirty-one, a thin man with a beard and a dark face. He
wears a blue kurta and is a worker in a garment factory. He is doing
work on piece rate and has taken a day off, not because it is a holiday,
but because this is his first free day for almost a month. He is feeling
'hot', as he says, and in need of release. He does not care whom he has
sex with today, a man, any man will do. He is feeling reckless.

His life is unbearably oppressive. He speaks of the long days sitting
in one position, cutting threads, sewing buttons, making buttonholes; a
long tedious labour from which the only distraction, he says, is his
thoughts, which no one can monitor. These are for much of the time
thoughts of home. Home and sex.

Anand's first sexual experience took place in a remote village on the border between Bihar and Orissa, where his family remain. As a child, he worked in the fields, looking after the buffaloes for the land-owner. 'One day, a neighbour was crossing the fields. It was the middle of the afternoon. It was very hot and everything was very quiet and still. He stopped where I was sitting under a rock, and asked me to go down with him and sit near the *nallah* [stream]. The riverbed was quite steep and almost dried up at that time of the year. We sat under a tree. I was nine or ten years old, I cannot remember exactly. This man sat down and took out his cock. He asked me to play with it. I knew this man and called him uncle, although he was not a relation of ours. He told me that if I rubbed it I would see something interesting. I did so until the *pani nikal aya* [he came].

'I knew nothing about this thing. My own was very small, and when I tried to do the same, nothing happened. It just felt very uncomfortable and I had to stop. But after that, it happened many times. When I was in the fields, he would pass by – always at the time of day when there was no one near. We would walk down to the river. Sometimes he put it in my mouth. That lasted for three or four years. The fields were lonely. I spent so many hours with the animals. They were my friends. They did not belong to us, they belonged to the land-owner, and this was my work from as long as I could remember.

'We had no land. We are Dalits. My cousin came to Delhi to work, and later he called me here. I was eighteen then. My parents did not want me to go, but we depend on work in other people's fields. I was very frightened of Delhi. I stayed with my cousin, but now I stay in the factory where I work, because this saves money. I send money home to my wife and two babies. My parents are both dead now, and we have a little better house than where I grew up. But we still live outside the village. We have our own well, so we have never had any trouble with upper castes. We are their workers. The neighbour who taught me sex, he is now an old man. When I go home, I go to see him. He is my good friend. We share a secret, and that is what binds people to each other.'

I was talking with Ganesh, one of the semiprofessionals in the Park. We were discussing whether it was possible for men to have sexual relationships in the rural areas. 'Of course,' he said. 'When I go home to my village in central UP I regularly have sex with my brother-in-law. In fact, in Delhi I am always passive, but when I go home I sleep with him and penetrate him. He has never been away from UP. We do not talk about it. It just happens. They have only two rooms and I sleep with him, while my sister sleeps with the children. She knows nothing, and we never discuss such things. It is only when two men are sleeping together, the warmth of the blood will make you feel like enjoying. This has happened for five years. He is happy with his wife, but when he sees me, he is happy also.'

The story of Praful, who was abused by a neighbour from the age of eight, also suggests that opportunities for illicit same-sex relationships are not rare in rural India. He says, 'I knew it was wrong, but I never said anything to anyone, because it was the normal way of things, that adults could do as they wished with children.'

It is one of the consequences of highly authoritarian and patriarchal societies that women and children are utterly in the power of men. To argue, as many fundamentalists, traditionalists and Gandhian radicals in India do, that 'Indian values' offer some kind of bulwark against 'decadent Western practices' such as child abuse, free sex and homosexuality, could not be more wrong. All they are doing is ensuring that such things will continue in secrecy and silence, and that children and women will be condemned to suffer. Praful says, 'I knew there was nothing I could do about it. Who would believe a child anyway against the word of a man, a householder and respectable citizen who keeps his family under his complete control?'

Jyoti is also from a village in Uttar Pradesh, not far from the border with Madhya Pradesh. Now twenty-four, he had his first sexual experience when he was sixteen. 'The boys used to play together; we were always playing cricket or chasing each other, running races. Our life was very physical. We roamed over the country whenever we had time from work and school. Most of us were child labourers, that is, we helped with the harvest, followed the animals, transplanted the rice, gathered fodder.

'I have two sisters, both older than I. We had five *bighas* of land, which my mother used to cultivate. We were told our father had gone away to Jabalpur for work; but we never saw him. When we grew older and asked our mother about him, she said, "Oh, he is dead."

'Most of the boys dropped out of school by the age of twelve or thirteen. Although our families were poor, we had a good life while we were growing up. We were happy with very small things, and we would kill hares and quails and even small monkeys which we took back home to eat; we would fish in the *nallahs* and gather leaves for medicine. We went swimming in the rainy season. It was only natural that we were curious about each other's bodies. It was just part of the fun of life. We knew that we were expected to work, which we did, although we had an easier time than the girls of the same age.

'There was one older boy, he was nineteen at this time. He was planning to go into the army. He was handsome, good at sport and everybody admired him. He didn't really move around with us, because he used to get up at four o'clock in the morning to take the milk from small farmers to the market in the town. One day, he took me with him. When we had finished, we stopped at a little *dhaba* [food-stall] on the road to eat something. That was the first time I tasted Coca Cola. I didn't like it. Afterwards, we left our bicycles in the road and walked over the grass. We lay down under a tree. He put his head in my lap, and I could feel myself getting hard. He took my penis into his mouth. Then I did the same to him. It was very good. I felt sad because he was going away, but before he went we used to go every other day, and he also penetrated me.

'He used to come home from Calcutta, where he was posted. He used to take a journey of thirty-two hours by train just to spend two or three days with me, so that we could be together. No one knew anything about what we did. My family thought he was a good friend to me, and they used to say, "Oh, he loves Prakash. Prakash is like his elder brother." They thought he was a good influence on me. And I did. I loved him, more than a brother. But when he left, I always used to cry. And I longed for him to come back. In the end, I grew tired of waiting for him, and I decided to come to Delhi. I just came by train one day. I had no ticket. I knew no one in Delhi. On my first day, I met a boy who sold toys in Connaught Place, and he got me my first job. I had sex with him as well. He lived with two other boys in Gole Market, and I shared the room with them; and when we were there alone, we would do it.

'I've sold calculators on the street; I sold soft toys; I sold old clothes from dead people; I worked for a tent company putting up *shamianas* [tents] for weddings and parties. Now I have a regular job in a bakery. I've met boys and men all over the city, and a lot of them are ready to do sex, if you get them in the right mood. I've learned a lot. I've even been a professional in Central Park. Soon I will go home to be married, but I will come back to Delhi. I cannot go back to live. There is no work and no excitement. I enjoy life. I have many friends. If ever there is trouble with the police, I always know half a dozen people who will lend me the money to pay them off.'

Those who attempt to integrate this experience more fully within their lives tend to do so as gay men, following a Western model of identity politics. A sizeable minority, however, were not entirely happy with this foreign version of male-to-male relationships and tried to express what they felt in terms of indigenous Indian experience. This is a not entirely successful effort, but it represents a reluctance to accept uncritically all the promptings that come from the West.

VIII

Rashid from near Gorakhpur in Uttar Pradesh confirms that there is indeed a tradition of Indian male-to-male relationships, untouched by

Western definitions and influences: 'In the village, sex between men does happen, but mainly if you know each other from youth. I know of some who started when they were children or young men, and they carry on after marriage. Otherwise, it is very difficult to meet others with the same interest. The only time is when there are weddings and many strangers come together. Sometimes they will sleep with each other, and then it happens. They will not tell, they will not say anything, and the next day they will go back to wherever they came from. It is forgotten immediately afterwards or at least is never spoken of, which comes to the same thing.'

Vishwanath from Wardha in Maharashtra says that he seduced his teacher when he was fifteen and maintained a relationship with him for five years. He says, 'I used to go for tuitions. He taught me Marathi and English. I knew what I was going to do. My Marathi and my English were both very good. I had no need of tuitions. He knew it and I knew it. We sat close over the textbook, and I pressed myself to him. Nothing was ever spoken. We just did it. He was not married at that time, although he did marry during the time I was having sex with him. Nothing was said. Nothing changed, he carried on with his job, and we carried on having sex. The only thing was, we didn't do it in his room any more. We had to go outside and meet away from town. It made it a little more difficult. It stopped because we had both had enough. Nothing was said then either. I had stopping having tuitions, and we just didn't see each other any more. We are friends. We meet when I go home. We never talk about it. Sometimes, I think he does not remember. Or maybe he has another friend now. I felt quite safe, even when I set out to get him to have sex with me, because I thought no one would ever believe that a boy of fifteen could seduce a man of twenty-six. But that is what happened.'

Saleem, in his early forties, says that he had heard of male-to-male relationships in his village in Bihar, although he had no direct experience there. There was one example that everyone talked of, where a man raped a boy. It came to be known and he was mutilated by the village people. 'It was not my own village, but about fifteen kilometres away. The boy was about twelve, and he complained to his father, and the family went to this man, who denied it. But the boy was very upset, and he had been injured; so when the doctor saw it, he said this must have been caused by some instrument or by the penis of a grown man. Some relatives of the boy went with other people from the village in the night and they took the man from his house. They were going to kill him. His wife and children begged for mercy, but the crowd took him and they castrated him. He survived, but it is still remembered to this day, even though it happened long ago.'

Samir used to take truck rides from his village into the cities of Uttar Pradesh when he was fifteen or sixteen: 'I was hitchhiking one day, and I was picked up by a truck carrying vegetables to Kanpur. That was a journey of about ten hours. It grew dark, and the driver said he was going to park the truck and sleep for the night, and I could stay with him if I wanted to. He had come from Gujarat, and he told me he had a wife and a son of my age. In the night he fucked me. I didn't like it, but I liked being close to a man; I liked his body, and he put his arm round me as we slept. He offered me a job as a helper, on condition that I would let him fuck me. I was confused. I knew that this was what I had been wanting. This was why I had stood on the highway looking for rides in the trucks that passed. I had these dreams about men, and I used to look at the trucks passing by and I imagined that one of them would stop and take me off, I don't know where. When it actually happened, I was quite shocked, because it was not at all as I had imagined. I had not thought of it so crude: he got out his cock and spat on his hands, then rubbed it on his cock; then took down my pants and entered me. It was not what I had thought of at all. So when he offered me the chance to stay with him, I said no. He set me down on the road and waved goodbye. When the truck drove away, I regretted it, and I wanted him to come back. I stood there, tears on my face, wanting him to turn round and come back. After that, when I went home, I used to stand by the highway for hours looking for this man, looking for his truck. I can remember it clearly, it was painted brown with red and green flowers all over the front. I never saw him again.'

The sexuality of truckers is a familiar theme, and not only in India: associated with a kind of casual mobility that suggests irresponsibility, acts without consequence, the nowhere road between localities, and not, therefore, bound by the moral laws of place-bound communities. It is not surprising that the recklessness of truck-drivers finds an echo in India, with the number of accidents that litter the highway – overturned vehicles, tangles of burnt-out metal, bodies covered with tarpaulin sheets by the side of the road. Brothels have sprung up on some of the truck routes; chains of small towns have found a new economic purpose in servicing them; and sexually transmitted diseases as well as AIDS have spread in their wake. That truckers – many of whom habitually abuse country liquor and drugs – should also not be squeamish about their sexual exploits leads to considerable male-to-male activity.

Ganesh is twenty-six. He came from Bihar, where his family is landless, three years ago to earn money in Delhi. He is the eldest of six brothers and sisters. He is a small wiry man, and when driving his cycle-rickshaw, he wears a check Madras cloth around his head, a threadbare lungi and a T-shirt that is full of holes. He pedals barefoot. His eyes are bright and fierce, but his appearance is deceptive. He is a gentle, even sad man. He says he will never be able to marry, because he has a deformed cock of which he is very ashamed: it is small and bent at an angle, and he dare not show it to people for fear they will laugh. He likes to be penetrated, but he tries to conceal what he thinks of as his deformity. He is drawn to men because, he says, he does not think he will be able to have sexual relations with a woman. When he was a child, he says, he did not know he had this abnormality. One day at school some other boys caught sight of him and they mocked him. He wanted to be like them and became obsessed with men and their cocks. At seventeen, he ran away from home. He was picked up on the road by a truck, whose driver took him on as a helper and used him sexually. That lasted a year. One day, they came to Delhi, and he decided to stay.

In such testimonies, there is a glimpse of the closed, concealed worlds of sexual practice in India, which remain untouched by ideas of being gay, identity politics or liberation; unacknowledged encounters bring release, sometimes affection, between strangers engaged upon what seems like a perpetual restless migration between town and city, between village and farm, in search of livelihood and survival. The embattled and secret lives of the men who are drawn to their own sex remain largely inaccessible, apart from the kind of brief insight we gain here. What people do is not integrated with what they say but remains separate, sometimes symbolised by the divided worlds of village and city, of home and outside. The Park is a kind of haven from daily conventions and the places in which family and work are located. People can be seen to change their behaviour at the exit; another demeanour and a different face are presented to the world, as visible as a change of costume.

Does this, therefore, mean that the Park represents a locus of integration, of harmony in otherwise discordant and divided lives? Not really. Most men expressed dissatisfaction with the management of their sexuality and the way this had to be accommodated in their lives. The overwhelming complaint was that the kind of relationships available in this marginal place, as indeed in most of the other cruising grounds of Delhi, were not really what they wanted. I was struck by the number of people who said with longing that what they would like above everything else was the opportunity to make love in comfort, without being hurried, in a bed with all their clothes off. A modest enough wish, one might think; yet impossible for the majority of men in Delhi, who must seize the opportunities that are offered for a moment of relief and release. Above all, the objection is to the quality of the relationship; and although there is a sizeable minority who claim that the release is functional and sufficient, many more say that they could wish for deeper relationships, something more lasting, a different quality of friendship from what is available.

I asked each man whether he preferred sex with women or men.

Prefer women:	10
Prefer men:	39
Fifty-fifty:	18
No preference expressed:	8

These responses are not necesssarily very reliable and should be taken only as a rough indication. For one thing, I spoke to all the men in a place where they were looking for same-sex relationships. It might, therefore, appear to be denying the obvious if they were to insist too much on their preference for women. The relatively high percentage who stated that they enjoyed sex equally with men and women – 24 per cent – may be an indication of a reluctance to say that they preferred or liked men exclusively; and this in itself may be unreliable, because many of the unmarried men had never had any sexual experience with women at all. However, none of them said he could not answer the question; and many stressed that they were confident that they would stop having sex with men after marriage, even though the testimonies of the married men suggest that these intentions may well not be maintained.

What was clear was the power of male friendships, and a pervasive longing for something more than the rough encounters in the Park.

Tushar says, 'Sex with men is easier than sex with women – easier to find, that is. It is safe, no problems. But what you get is release. It is *jaldi sex, khatam* [quick sex, then it is finished]. People go back to their wives, their lives. I would like to have a friend to spend some time with, to get to know him, to make real friendship and to enjoy at leisure.'

Mr Manek likes sex with men, but he is repelled by the crude and mechanical experiences that he finds among pick-ups in Delhi: 'What I would like above anything else is to have a friend, with whom to share everything and to enjoy in peace. In the random sexual encounters here there is little affection, little exploration of mutual interests, virtually no emotional, spiritual or intellectual content; yet these things are vital in the lives of all of us. Such meetings leave you depressed rather than satisfied, discontented rather than uplifted. Yet in Delhi opportunities for meeting people do exist, as in other metropolitan cities, in ways that are simply not possible in the smaller towns and villages, where, after all, a majority of the people of India live. So you have to accept what is possible. But still I dream that I may meet some younger person to whom I could act as guide or even father: take him under my wing, offer him protection, contribute to the formation of his sensibility and character. That, at least, remains my wish and my hope, even though now I am in my forties I suppose I should no longer expect too much.'

Paras Ram, twenty-two and still experimenting with sex and relationships, says he is looking for 'friendship'. His only experience with men before coming to the Park was with school and college friends, which none of them had taken seriously. 'We used to play with one another, but it was not really friendship, just time-pass.' Paras Ram becomes romantically attached to one young man after another he meets in the Park. He is to be seen holding hands or sitting on the grass with his head in his friend's lap. He says he wants a relationship with a man in which sex is not necessarily the main purpose. 'I do not know whether I want full sexual relations with him or not. All I want is affection. Maybe sex will come, I do not know; but I want someone I can talk to, to whom I can tell everything that is in my heart. Here, as soon as people have done sex together they lose interest in one another. I don't like that.'

Samir would like 'a permanent friend. I know many people who come here regularly, but they are looking only for immediate sexual enjoyment. When you come here and talk to them they will be friendly enough. They will sit and talk. But all the time they are looking over your shoulder, to see who has come; and if they see someone they think is more interesting, they will leap up and run away. There are many people who will not do with the same person twice. So the second time you see them, they shake your hand and move on.'

Harish is very lonely in Delhi: 'Of course there are so many people here, you can make contact for sex very quickly. But that is not what I want. I want love, but especially someone to take care of me. Sometimes I go to Nehru Park. There, people meet in the darkness. They do not even see one another properly, let alone make a friendship. All they want is sex, then finish and go away, pretend it does not happen. There is no continuity, no follow-up, no friendship. I am very vulnerable because I fall in love with people who show an interest in me, and then I get hurt. I have two friends in particular and they call me when they are alone and wanting sex; but when I am needing company or affection they never think of calling me.'

Pandu says, 'I prefer to have one friend to stay with permanently. I do have a boyfriend now, but he is a businessman, and he is always busy or travelling out of Delhi. I have to call him up and make arrangements when he is free, at his convenience. But that is India: you cannot think of living together, or making a home, of staying in the same place. Even if you are committed to someone, you have to make your life in secret.'

Pandu, who is a very attractive man, adds, 'Being good-looking does not make life easy. People see you and they say immediately, "I love you"; but they have no idea who this "you" they are talking about is. They are drawn to your face or your body, but they do not know, and often they do not care, what kind of a person you are. No one looks behind the appearance of things. I don't like this, and I pay no attention when people say they love me.'

LOVE IN A DIFFERENT CLIMATE

'I am looking for commitment,' says Rohan. 'I have many friends, but none with whom I can think of making a life together. I am looking desperately for such a relationship, even though I know that when you are desperate, you rarely find it. It often comes when you least expect it, when you are not searching too hungrily. I have had a number of relationships with men, I have seen one man on a regular and exclusive basis; but somehow it always breaks up. Maybe this is India; the social pressure is so great that individual relationships cannot survive it. It all has to be secret and in isolation from the rest of your social life, so that it cannot stand the strain. . . . It is the opposite of marriage, which is a public statement and is at the centre of all social activity. Everything supports marriage, but nothing is there to strengthen friendships between men.'

'I need love more than sex,' declares Girish. 'The men in Nehru Park, they do sex in the dark and lead their other life in the daylight. I want a long-term friend with whom I can be open, someone I can love and cherish. I do not know whether this is possible or just a dream.'

What Rashid really wants is 'sex in a bed, no clothes, *aram se* [in comfort], taking it easy, then sleeping together with your legs wrapped around each other and in his arms. It doesn't happen very often, but I dream about it. . . . If you have a place of your own, if you have privacy in India, I think you can get almost anyone to come with you, whoever you are. Friendships here are in the Park only; they finish at the bus stand outside. This place is like the zoo – sex in captivity.'

'You do not make friends with the people,' says Man Singh, speaking of the men in the Park. 'You see the same boys. You can talk to them, laugh and share a joke, you can have sex, but you cannot think seriously about friendship. For most people here, their real life is outside – their family life, their work, their social life is not flexible. There is no space in Indian society to accommodate such things as homosex. Coming here is for a few hours' relaxation only. People do not want relationships that are too deep or that will demand too much of them – that is exactly what a lot of them are running away from. They are suffocated by their families. So do not look for anything that will survive once you go out from here; you will only be disappointed.'

Premchand says friendship is for him the most important relationship: friendship is important for young men because they cannot talk openly with their fathers. 'Boys can talk to each other, find comfort and security with each other. They can tell what is in their heart and feel it is safe. No one is going to challenge them. They can experiment with sex with each other. Boys of the same age-group stay together, play with each other's bodies, compare their cocks. . . . Then, when they are older, they forget about it. They become like their fathers, distant and aloof, and they do not remember how it was for them. And then their sons have to find out about life on their own. . . . It isn't so easy to find that kind of friendship when you are an adult. I am hungry for love, and I know that such relationships are hard to find in Delhi.'

Ram Singh had a five-year relationship with a man from the north of Ireland when he was posted in Bangalore. 'I was 27 when we met, and that changed my life. . . . Now that is finished and I miss it very much. I always wanted a relationship with an older man. I still would like one. I do not mind if he is seventy or eighty. I like kissing, I like affection, not just the act of sex. I picked up a man yesterday and took him to the hotel where I'm staying. It was not very interesting. He just wanted to come and then leave as soon as he could. It is as though he wanted to get it over with quick, quick, so he could forget and then deny he does this. There is no conversation, no show of affection. He goes away satisfied, but I am left lonely and frustrated. Maybe he has his wife to go to for all the love and affection he wants.

'When I was younger, I would have loved a relationship with an older man. Perhaps it was because I had a father who lived under the shadow of death. He was an invalid throughout all my childhood and died of TB when I was fourteen. He never belonged to this world because of his illness. I always knew he would leave us, and, as a child, you cannot permit your feelings to get tangled with those you know will die, it is too painful. . . .

'I think many young men are as I was. If you are forty or fifty years old, you can become a father to them. Many young men have no father they can talk to, because the older generation does not understand. If a youngster has nocturnal discharges, if he has something that happens naturally, say a fungal infection in the penis, he will not dare to talk to his father about this. And even if he does, the father will be embarrassed and will not know what to say.'

Manohar says longingly, 'I would prefer a relationship that continues, one that lasts longer than the casual meetings with people here. Of course you make friends, you find people to share with and talk to. I want only one person to be a special friend. I have my family, and I love them. I do not think there is room enough in our human heart for more than three or four people. Our people live very crowded lives, but the family crowds the heart as much as the house where we live. There is little feeling left over. But if you have a relationship with another man, he is brother, friend, father, lover. You can always find room for something you desire very much – a special friendship, someone to share everything with, from whom there are no secrets and you love unto death. That is what I wish for.'

Mowla Ao, who comes to the Park whenever he has time from work, says that most of all he values friendship: 'Above everything, I like to talk to people. If they are good, I like them. Just for friendship, as we are talking now. That is also a relief from loneliness. Sometimes it can be a greater relief than sex, which may ease you physically, but can leave you feeling more lonely than before.

'If I am gay or not I do not know what it means. One day soon I will go home and get married. . . . When I come here, I see the same people, and we will sit for an afternoon like this. I do not tell them my real name or my work. I only give my telephone number when I know someone very well. There is anonymity here, which I like because there is no commitment. Of course I dream of finding someone I will love and who will love me, but I do not think this is the place where I will find him; yet if I cannot find him here, I do not know where else in India I should look.'

Vikram is in his early thirties. He wears a frayed baseball cap, white sneakers, dark red check trousers. He works in a factory making plastic vessels and earns three thousand rupees a month. He has a wife and two children. He has come here, *'ghumne'*, he says, a word that implies strolling and relaxation, roaming around. During the course of the afternoon, I saw him wandering through the scrubland, patrolling the sparse vegetation of the jungle area, a portly melancholy figure. Towards evening, he came and sat beside me once more. By now he was very dejected. 'Nothing,' he said. *'Khali. Bekhar.'* 'What are you looking for?' I asked. He said, 'Friendship.' It seems such a simple thing, and yet it remains elusive. He looked at me forlornly and said, 'Sex with a man is good.' Then he added, 'A man knows what another man likes.' This is an old story; versions of it appear in many societies. 'But, surely, women know what men like.' 'How can they?' he retorted. 'They are women.' It sounded logical. He said, 'A man knows what it is like to be sucked, and because of that, a man knows how to do it. Women cannot know.' Impatient with what he must have perceived as the dullness of my comprehension, he rose and walked out of the Park.

His account of what he was doing seemed to open up more questions than it resolved. It suggested interesting erotic depths to the notion of same-sex friendship and a more fluid concept of men being together than that which is conveyed by the Western labels 'gay' or 'bisexual', which appeared to me – not for the first time – reductive when set beside the more complex and less formulaic versions of what the Indian men in the Park were looking for. These, for all their evasions and denials, hint at something less knowable, less definable than the prosaic and precise terminology of the West claims to reveal. On the other hand, the difficulties for men in India to pursue such relationships leaves them far more in the realm of abstraction, of unfulfilled possibility. At least men in Europe and the US live together, they live out relationships, for good or ill, which is something their Indian counterparts rarely achieve. It may be that the fluidity of Indian male-to-male relationships endows them with a sense of perpetual anticipation, which doesn't get used up or worn out in the actual day-to-day pressure of living together.

The relative lack of availability of same-sex relationships in India surrounds them with a romantic halo, which is partly responsible for making people say that they would like to leave India, to live in the West, where such attachments may become ordinary and play themselves out like any other relationship. However, it is clear that those who do have the opportunity for deeper love-relationships find that they also stumble against the conventions of straight models, against the reluctance – or fear – of men to commit themselves to each other. Rajesh, twenty-seven, tells this story of friendship.

'I have one man who, I am sure, loves me. He is a very close friend, although we never had sex. Although he cares for me very deeply, he is always quarrelling with me, arguing with me, punishing me. It is because he is himself gay, and he is fighting it within himself. So when he is fighting with me, it is against himself that he is struggling, because I am openly gay. He wants to deny it in himself, and that is why he is always attacking me. He sees himself as strong and me as weak. Yet this is not really the way it is. He cannot bear it because in fact I am very strong, probably stronger than he is; yet I am the gay one and ought to be feeble and womanish. Whenever I go with a woman, which I sometimes do, he becomes very angry and jealous. One day, he even called his mother and said to her, "See, this man is following me everywhere, he is a homosexual." After that, I said to him, "All right then, you sever all connection with me. We will not meet again. Stop seeing me completely." He then attacked me physically, kicked me and hit me. Then he goes. After that, he is on the telephone, fifteen, twenty times, begging me not to break our friendship. I think he loves me too much, but he cannot let himself see it, let alone admit it to me. I am to be married in October. My fiancée is a good girl, a computer operator. I will not tell her. What good will it do? I have to be married, because my only brother died in January. He was thirty-three and also unmarried. I have one married sister. But my parents are still grieving badly over the death of my brother. I have no choice but to be married, and that is no hardship to me. My brother died of kidney failure: they gave him an injection in the hospital that went terribly wrong. He had pneumonia, and the injection they gave him killed him.

'When I told my friend I am to be married, he was very angry. He said, "I will come with you and your wife for your honeymoon." He said, "We will take a drink, and I will fuck her, then she will become pregnant and our lives will be mingled in blood." Why would he say a thing like that? One day, he went with a prostitute. Well, she isn't really a prostitute, but she is ready to have sex with men for money. Later, I met this woman, and she told me he never did anything but talk. He cannot bear it that I am the stronger and he is weak. I am supposed to be gay and he is supposed to be straight. I think the truth is he cannot do it with a woman and is afraid to do it with a man. He wants to see himself as male and me as female. He cannot believe it when I say I want to make love to a woman. His pride and self-respect prevent him from telling me that he loves me, so he tries to control me all the time.'

IX

The dense web of family relationships and the relentless nature of work in India combine to act both as screen and as protection for many Indian men. It is difficult to distinguish individual needs from the over-powering structures of convention; and the absence of welfare provision outside the family is a powerful inhibitor of efforts to transcend it. The stories the men tell are of meeting themselves by surprise, as it were, discovering their sexuality by the pressure of another's body at random, when they are least expecting it.

It is easy to see this as 'repression', to dismiss it as the result of an 'undeveloped' or socially 'backward' society. Indeed, even some of those who have easily acknowledged their sexuality are dismissive of those who really do not know themselves and claim this is only a form of play-acting and pretence. One gay-identified man says, of what he sees as the pseudo-innocence of those who insist that only when some event aroused their consciousness, did they gain the knowledge of their liking for men, 'Of course they know. Only they will not say. They do not wish to admit that they are gay, so they say someone else forced them into it. What have they been doing all their lives, sleepwalking? It is impossible not to know, as impossible as not knowing that your eyes are brown or your skin black.' This response is not uncommon among the better-off gay men, the English-speaking minority who find an affinity with gay politics and solace in the advance of Western categories of understanding and interpreting what it means to have sex with men.

But this is too simple; it is itself a response of the powerful, those who have had access to Western liberal education, who know global English-language culture. To the powerless it can appear crushing, dominant and oppressive. Another man, less dogmatic, said, 'Indians do this thing, but they don't talk about it. They don't give it a name, and then it is OK. It is integrated into life not in theory, but as it is lived and experienced. Once you start to rationalise and explain, it becomes something else, and that something else falsifies the Indian form of integration. In this way, even your liberation can become another form of colonialism. That is what you have to avoid.'

Satya, who is a painter in his fifties, affirms that 'Indian sexuality is traditionally amorphous and that many gods partake of both male and female characteristics. They are protean, take the shape of one or the other, now male, now female, which itself symbolises the dualism of human sexuality. For instance, one of the forms of Vishnu is Ardhanarishwar, which means "half-female god". This duality is accepted in Indian philosophy, in the same way that other dualities coexist: creation and destruction, which exist side by side, the figure and the abstraction. The gods are represented in abstract or human form. In sexuality, as long as the dualism remains ambivalent, complementary, there is no problem. Only when things come to be categorised, as in Article Three hundred and seventy-seven of the Penal Code, which speaks of "acts against the order of nature", it takes on a crude physicality, concentrating on the sexual act rather than on the whole affective and emotional complexity that goes with being male or female, or any combination of them, along a continuum that knows nothing of such abrupt breaks.

'This is what colonialism did, and what the framers of the colonial laws did. It was a violence to Indian tradition and culture, and we are still living with it. The arrival of your gay liberation or your gay-straight-bisexual categories only continues that process of distorting our Indian tradition and imposing something alien upon it. You have no right to march through the world reshaping all cultures in your own image and calling it human nature. It tells much more about the nature of Western mania with naming and pigeonholing human phenomena than it does about the nature of humanity. You want to make Western man or woman or gay or lesbian into universal man, woman, gay or lesbian. It is a kind of cultural terrorism and we must resist it. In India, to be a friend may have erotic overtones or it may not. If a male friend comes to visit a married couple, the wife will leave the marriage bed to the friend. There may be sex or there may not. That is not the point. But they will say, "Oh, he cannot sleep alone, he may be lonely or he may feel unwelcome. His friend must be there to make him comfortable". The wife will sleep with the children or her mother. It will not necessarily matter to her if sex takes place between the men – even if she knows it – because this does nothing to undermine her place at the heart of the family.'

Karim, a historian from Lucknow, was also eloquent on the same issue. Karim is from an old landed family, his grandfather was educated at Cambridge and his father became a senior government bureaucrat. His father enjoyed shooting tigers and migratory birds and ducks with

English guns, a mixture of Indian Brahmin and colonial English gentleman. All three of his children became academics.

Karim is alienated by Western identity-politics. He believes that it overlays and effaces much within the Indian tradition of same-sex relationships. 'Some of the Urdu poets, for instance, wrote about a whole network of people living at that time, and a clear picture emerges of the relationships between them. You can tell what they are saying from the words they use, although it is nowhere spelled out. The eighteenth century is the period I know best, and that is restricted to north India, so I would be unwilling to generalise. But in that century, there is much mention of same-sex relationships. In Delhi in the mid-eighteenth century – Shahjahanabad, as it then was, now Old Delhi – men would meet and walk hand in hand, and retreat to the *gahwa khanas* around the Chandni Chowk for tea and poetry. Beautiful youths were celebrities as dancers and singers; one always dressed in white and danced in front of the main gate of Red Fort. Mir Kallu had elaborate parties where he entertained his friends and their beloveds with music and liquor in the privacy of tents. Love between members of the same sex was portrayed as a higher form of attraction and was even considered divine by some. Both the poets Amir and Abru were known by everyone to love men, and this never affected their standing as poets. We should try to retrieve our history, which is the memory of our difference. We have to validate and reclaim it, not follow Western models which, however appropriate for them, only cloud our own past and cut us off from it.

'Historically, at least as far as men were concerned, as long as you continued the lineage, no one really cared what else you did. And you will find this attitude still deeply rooted in many Indian men today. They must get married and have children; that is a duty which cannot be avoided. But what they do beyond that is not subject to scrutiny, as long as they are discreet. It is a perfectly effective and civilised way of managing human sexuality.

'Only in the nineteenth century silence falls on all this, coinciding with the consolidation of British rule. The infamous Article Three hundred and seventy-seven is only one aspect of a much wider moral code in force at that time.

'It is a historical paradox that those who say to me "Why do you not come out?" are nearly all Westerners or Indians living in the West. I have felt no need or wish to do so. On the other hand, I have remained unmarried, but I have nevertheless received much support of all kinds from my family. Many gay people of my generation would not have survived without our families. A lot of young Indians who are eager to proclaim that they are gay have not thought very deeply about these things. In the same way, I was shocked when I lived in North America to find how many gay people repudiate the family as an ideology. In India this would scarcely be possible, and anyone foolish enough to proclaim it will soon come up against the reality that it is only through family that security and protection can be found against sickness, old age and adversity; without the family, they will soon learn about life on the hard city pavements.'

Relatively few in Indian are committed to a specifically Indian way of expressing same-sex relationships. As Karim suggests, much of the knowledge of this has been eroded by colonial rule and has been rediscovered in the context of the market economy, which is the contemporary form of Western dominance and a symptom of the spread of its universalising mission in the world. Yet this question still haunts many discussions about change in India: liberation, liberalisation or modernisation?

Shivananda Khan, Calcutta-born founder of NAZ in London and a tireless researcher into sexual identities in South Asia, points out that a compelling reason now exists for not projecting onto India Western concepts of straight, gay and bisexual: the spread of AIDS cannot be prevented by having recourse to these stereotyped and rigid categories. Men who have sex with men do not recognise themselves in these classifications, and any attempt to reach them and to create consciousness of the need for safer sex will not reach them. Shivananda Khan speaks of the diversity of male-to-male relationships: the married auto-rickshaw driver who has occasional sex with men; the married hotel worker who pays a female sex worker once a month and also has sex with men in the hotel; the male prostitute at the station who says he enjoys his work; the married businessman who occasionally cruises in the parks; the two illiterate sweepers who have lived together for five years.

'These are not gays, they do not see themselves as bisexual, yet neither are they conventionally straight. Of course, in India there are lesbian and gay identities, but these are confined chiefly to the emerging middle class, [which] is a product of urban industrialised and commercial culture, with its sense of individualism and privacy. Gay activism is now challenging the legal framework in which homosexuality was conceived by the Raj. But it does not touch the more than eighty per cent of people in India who live in villages, who do not speak English and whose identities are overwhelmingly constructed around the individual's position in the joint family, kinship networks, marriage and children. Concepts of a personal self separated from the others are weak; all this seriously modifies and influences actual sexual behaviours.

'Marital relationships and procreative sex are a primary duty for men. Those who would prefer relationships with men may look outside marriage for emotional satisfaction, or they may seek sexual pleasure or release outside. They may find significant satisfaction within the family matrix, but need occasional contact with men. Others, especially before a marriage that may be delayed to the age of thirty or beyond, or if the sexual relationship with their wife is not fulfilling, seek external encounters, may look for occasional male contacts; while young men, especially among the poorer classes, often just play around for fun and do not invest their activities with any great significance.

'The import of Western concepts also destroys Indian traditions of friendship: indigenous homoaffective and homosocial relationships are destroyed under the withering blast of being labelled "gay". Indigenous histories and cultures are effaced by what becomes a kind of sexual neo-colonialism, where even our deepest relationships are reshaped in the image of Western ideas of straight, gay and bisexual.'

Jagdish, a non-gay man from Assam, spoke with feeling about the nature of friendship between men in India: 'It is partly because the family is hierarchical and patriarchal that boys cannot speak to their parents, especially to their fathers, about things that cause them anxiety, things that trouble them as they are growing up. This makes them more dependent on each other to talk about what is in their heart. In that sense, friendship is a very solemn and serious thing, because friendship is forged as a kind of defence against the profoundest and most unbreakable relationship in the patriarchal tradition – that between father and son.

'The structures of authority lead you to respect your parents. You hold them in high regard. But you cannot speak openly to them. They expect a great deal of you. They assume that you will live up to the highest standards, so you will only disappoint them if you speak to them of your weaknesses, your fears and your pain. This is especially true when it comes to matters of sex and relationships between men and women. For example, if an adolescent boy gets a nocturnal emission from his penis, he will not dream of confessing this to his father, even less of taking advice from him. Instead, he will tell his friends or one friend he knows he can trust. That may also be a cousin or a brother or some other relative, but someone close to him in age and of the same status in the family. This is why friendship is often conflated with brotherhood: brothers, cousin-brother, friend-as-brother are all relationships that are sacred; and betrayal can lead to passionate enmity.

'And then, even when he is married, there may be similar inhibitions with his wife. He will still go to his friends to talk: if there is some sexual problem, he will not discuss with his wife but will wish to share experiences with his friends, compare feelings and find out if this is their experience too. He will also not wish to reveal his anxieties and weaknesses to his wife. Even if something is wrong in the marriage, he will take consultation from those he can trust. And this is accepted by everyone. It makes for some powerful bondings and creates loyalties that will not easily be broken.

'It is understood that relationships between men run deep; as indeed, they do between women. They entrust their deepest feelings to one another. It should not surprise us if those deepest feelings also become entwined with those of the friend.

'I wouldn't say that sex never occurs between such friends, particularly in the time when they are young and before they are married, but it may be just for discharge and in keeping with the intimacy of their friendship. That doesn't suggest that they are gay. It certainly isn't the reason for the depth of their friendship; this comes from the complete confidence and trust, born maybe out of necessity, but it binds them for life. Often a man will feel closer to his friend than to his wife, in the sense that they know each other's feelings and can anticipate one another's reactions. Friendship, in this sense, is a very significant thing. I wouldn't know whether it is more profound than it is in other cultures, but it has a special role in the lives of Indian men.'

Satya, who spends his time between London and his village in his native Bengal, also spoke of friendship between men in general rather than between men who have sex with each other. He said, 'I have found friendship in the West to be shallow and instrumental. In other words, people befriend one another for what they can get out of you. Since I have been in London, I have helped many young scholars, people going to India for the first time. I have offered them advice and contacts, and have given them an introduction to India, as it were. In the first instance, they are eager to come and listen; but after they have taken what they want, you never hear from them again. Some have later become quite prominent. But they have never thanked me or even, in many cases, contacted me again. This used to hurt and shock me. Now, of course, I'm used to it. People have surrounded me here [in London] whenever I have been successful; but when I am lonely or in need, they are absent. On the other hand, friends I have from my village have remained constant, and whenever I go home, they will come to meet me. They are always open and ready to welcome me. Here, you have to telephone and make bookings with friends, it is more like business appointments; whereas in India it is the availability of friends that strikes you.

'I realise that this is, in part, a consequence of the increased pace of life in the West, the mobility and busyness which dominate people's lives. Indian friendships are still a product of greater rootedness and stability. No doubt all this will change, is changing, under the impact of development. But for the present, we still have the benefits of lives that may be narrow geographically – the majority of people in India still do not travel far from their place of birth, in spite of the migration to the cities – but they gain in depth.'

This is the view of a man attached to his origins, whose local roots have nourished and informed his writing and painting.

A quite different view of male relationships came from a dancer and a writer whom I met in Delhi. Both have lived in the West. They identify as gay and, indeed, were lovers for several years and still maintain a close friendship.

We are in Lodhi Garden on a warm evening in March. Delhi is at its most magical. A full moon shines on the Lodhi tombs and winks on the muted blue ceramic of the Shish Gumbad; the red sandstone smoulders in the half-light. The scented air is filled with the cries of night birds, bats and flying foxes.

Harshad, the writer, has come back to India to write a book about the causes of its abiding poverty. This, he says, he feels he owes to his country, a country in which, however, he can no longer live and thrive. When he has finished the manuscript, he will return to the United States. Rohan, the dancer, lives in Kerala but performs all over the world, especially in Europe and America.

Both have flourished in the West and have found their talents recognised there in a way that simply does not happen in their country. They express disillusionment and disappointment with what they refer to as the instrumentalism and lack of affection of the Indian men with whom they have had sexual relations. It is significant that they use the same word that Satya applied to non-sexual friendships in the West.

'Indian men are often crude and coarse in their sexual approach. You see a divine-looking boy, and you think he must be the most sensitive soul on earth. But all he wants to do is put his cock in your mouth, to come and go, without even taking his clothes off.' Rohan denies there is any erotic quality in relationships between Indian men. 'Eroticism depends upon respect between people, and here this does not exist. . . . People want to service you or be serviced. This is not erotic.'

Harshad tells how, while he was researching his book, his car broke down in a remote spot in Uttar Pradesh. 'I was miles from anywhere and despaired of getting to my destination. Eventually, a boy on a motorbike stopped, about nineteen, dazzling smile. He was angelic. He helped me repair the car and got it going. I told him I was from Delhi and he asked if he could see me again. I gave him my address, not expecting that our paths would ever cross. A few weeks later, without warning, he turned up. I was both astonished and delighted. But my pleasure didn't last long. It was a very disappointing encounter. He stayed only ten minutes. No preamble. He just wanted to come, get it over, and then he couldn't wait to get away.'

Neither of the two men is impressed by my assertion that there is a powerful undertow of eroticism in relationships between Indian men: they see this as a form of cultural projection by Westerners upon what they perceive as crude and rudimentary sexual encounters. On the other hand, they themselves are impressed by what they perceive as the subtlety, richness and sense of equal status between gay men in the West. 'In India, there is no equality between people in such encounters. It is at best a patron-client relationship if you pick up some young man, and at worst a brief and unsatisfactory meeting.'

Perhaps we are all doomed to see things, or imagine that we see things, in that which is exotic, foreign, and other; and to set little value on what is close at hand, local and familiar. Certainly, on reflection, there was some misunderstanding in the discussion that was taking place: I was referring rather to the observable loyalties and affections between men in India of all ages – the physical closeness and holding of hands which causes so many Western visitors to believe, mistakenly, that being gay is a common and open experience in India; while they were speaking of the pick-ups which they, as privileged men, might make by chance. They were speaking of the possibilities that certainly do exist in the West for gay men to make long-term stable relationships and live together. They were looking at the situation from their own Westernised and socially advantaged position. In that sense, they are bearers of precisely those values which Karim and other Indians whose lives are anchored within India deplore. Yet there is truth in both testimonies.

Harshad explained more fully one of the significant moments which had made him realise that living as a gay man in India is not possible for him. '[Rohan and I] lived together for five years. Close to the apartment where we lived there was a couple, a married couple, who took violently against us and resented our presence in this apartment block. They complained to the police that we were committing illegal acts, acts against nature, in the words of the famous statute which your country bequeathed us. At first the police ignored it, but this couple insisted and became more and more shrill in their denunciations. We were finally questioned by the police. We told them it was a case of personal spite and the police went away. But they wouldn't let go. Later, we were arrested and placed in a police cell. Rohan is diabetic, and without insulin he will faint and fall into a coma. We were left, despite my protests, for several hours. I told them, "Look, this man will die." They were quite indifferent to it. It made me feel the arbitrariness of power in India, the cruelty of it. How brutal life is for the powerless, we got a taste of it then. They were quite impervious to reason and to humanity. Eventually, we were released, and I made a complaint against the police through a politician who knows my family. But of course nothing happened, no action was taken.

'It was the inflexibility of the police that was so frightening, their contempt for anyone who comes into their power. It was very chilling, and gave me a quite different insight into India. I have always known intellectually what life is like for the poor, but to be on the receiving end of it only reinforces the revulsion and anger. I don't want to stay here. I came back to write this book, in which I feel I am paying my debt to those I leave behind. But I would rather be in a place where I feel secure and comfortable with being gay. I am not going to jeopardise my wellbeing and throw away the opportunity to live as I want to for some sentimental principle of a patriotism which, in this sense, I do not feel.'

What became clear from these discussions is a confirmation of a commonplace – that there are two Indias: that of the well-to-do, which is articulated to an international culture of privilege, and that which is subject to traditional power-relationships, to a rooted culture, to the unchanging patterns of endurance and survival. The great majority of people will never have access to the former. Both have their strengths and disadvantages, which have been well-rehearsed. And these cultures are at war with one another; India is the terrain on which the struggle between traditional subsistence and survival confronts the modernising, consumerist values of the global economy. Of course, the latter is making headway on every front, as many of the men I spoke with were well aware.

Sandeep, university administrator and supporter of the fundamentalist Bharatiya Janata Party, says, 'In India, it is the upper classes who have become Westernised, and the lower classes remain with their traditions. We in the middle class have the worst time, because we are neither one thing nor the other. We have to decide which we want, which side we are on. This is why so many of us are turning back to tradition.'

The truth of Sandeep's observation is that the middle class, those emerging into the market economy, are torn between wanting to retain traditional identities and the lure of individual freedom, not to mention the attraction of all the good things the market can provide. The men in the Park reflected this struggle, some coming down on the side of modernisation and eagerly embracing the Western model of personal fulfilment; others emphatically seeking to conceal the complexity of their sexual needs by conforming outwardly and identifying strongly with traditional family structures.

Kamal, thirty-four, was trapped in a relentless hunt for sexual release until he discovered his own gayness. 'From early experience in college, I learned of the secret circles of men looking for sex with men. Once you learn that this exists, you can see it everywhere. You learn to make contact by the exchange of a split-second glance, the raising of an eyebrow, the lingering of a footstep, the searching look at a face, a way of walking. Signals that no else would ever pick up, but which are unmistakable once you are initiated. It is at the same time unseen but highly visible. But it doesn't get you relationships, friendship, love, respect or comfort. It gets you sex. It is only by discovering the existence of yet another world – the openly gay world where you are not bound by pretence or false machismo or the demands of family – that you come out into the free air of making real choices, deeper relationships, more satisfactory friendships with other men.'

This battle between tradition and modernisation – in this context, between hidden male-to-male relationships and openly avowed gay sexual orientation – sometimes sets up powerful and distressing conflicts within individuals.

Shailendra has been married for two years and has a daughter of nine months. He is passionately devoted to his wife, but the desire for men overcomes him from time to time and he is unable to resist it, even though this is what he wishes to do. He had imagined – like many others – that marriage would put an end to what he describes as his 'shameful desires'. Whenever he yields to his need for male contact, he comes to the Park with beating heart, in a state of high excitement – feverish, urgent, his mouth dry, his palms sweating. Afterwards, he feels self-hatred; and when he returns home to his wife, her artlessness and innocence and her joy at seeing him rekindle an even stronger sense of worthlessness in him, far worse than any blame or reproach would be. When he is in the Park, he cannot be free from thoughts of his wife; and when he is with her, he thinks of the men from the Park.

He has sex with her about three times a week, but uses the remembered images of men to achieve the necessary state of excitement. He has felt like this since college, perhaps even earlier, from the age of fourteen or fifteen, when boys in school used to play around together. Since then, he says, he has been waiting for it to pass, but it hasn't. Now, he says, it has become a nightmare. He is twenty-eight.

We sit and talk. I say that human sexuality is a mysterious thing, that we all occupy a place somewhere along a continuum from 100 per cent heterosexual to 100 per cent homosexual, although probably very few of us are in such extreme positions. There are elements of the opposite gender in most of us, even if that amounts to only 10 or 20 per cent. I say to him, 'Isn't sexual ambivalence part of the diversity of our life? It doesn't, and doesn't have to, affect your love for your wife.'

Shailendra says he never has sex twice with the same man, because he would not wish his feelings to become engaged with them, and he can never bear to see them again. They only remind him of what he sees as his own weakness. I say to him, 'Why don't you try to have a regular partner, a trusted friend?' He says it is precisely the anonymity of the stranger that creates the compulsion. He says it is man he wants, not a particular man, but someone who becomes, briefly, maleness itself for him, from whom he can take a kind of nourishment that will feed his own weak sense of male identity. He is, he declares, 'tormented by this struggle'.

I ask him if he would like to come to a gay support group in Delhi; and I give him the number of the helpline which is available two nights a week, if he should need to talk. I say, 'By talking to others, you'll come to know you are not alone with these feelings and conflicts. If you share them, you may come to accept something that is causing you such anguish.'

He will not accept and will not phone. 'I am not a gay,' he says indignantly, fiercely. Then, uncertain again, he asks, 'Shall I tell my wife?' He looks at me intently, clearly asking for guidance.

I hesitate. At one time, I would have said unequivocally yes. But if I have learned one thing, it is that reactions that may be culturally appropriate in the West may be quite the reverse in India. So I say, 'What could she do with that information? How will it help her? Will two unhappy people be better than one? If you think she could accept and understand that is one thing; but if it only estranges you, since you have no option for any other life, what purpose will be served?'

This is how the dividedness actually works itself out in the lives of individuals, where awareness of sexual orientation is at war with duty and tradition.

Mangesh, in his forties, also recognises the change that is sweeping India and catching up the middle classes in its convulsions. When we met, I asked him what his work is. He said, 'I am an agriculturalist.' Such a response was a sure indication that this is not his primary job. He is from Haryana, where he and his brother own seventy *bighas* of land. But he is also a teacher in a government school in Delhi, where he has worked for the past eighteen years. His wife is also a teacher. They have two boys, one at university, the other at school in the Ninth Standard.

He says, 'Human beings are not governed by reason, but by the heart. The need that takes possession of me every so often is quite irrational. I am happy with my wife. People will say that my desire for men is perverse and unnatural. These things are real, we are part of nature, so in that sense, of course, it is natural. Attraction to my own sex has always been in me. It is not something that came recently. Since adolescence, I was always drawn to other boys. It cannot be conquered by the power of will, which is why I say we are not controlled by

LOVE IN A DIFFERENT CLIMATE

reason. The problem is, of course, that in society you have to have controls and restraints. What happens beneath the surface is always turbulent, chaotic, contradictory, and it always threatens to break through the outer decorum. This is, to some degree, what is happening in India now. We have developed mechanisms for keeping this sexual force if not quiet, at least invisible, unspoken. So what is expected of people is one thing; and what they have done privately, secretly, is something else. But now we see the chaos emerging from beneath and setting itself up as new norms, because it is not really chaos: it is merely something which the society is afraid of and which it tries to suppress. But when this emerges into the light, it is not so terrible as it seemed when it was prohibited. After some time, it becomes accepted, absorbed into our lives, and we wonder why we were so afraid of it. Other things then will be forced into the darkness, new taboos and prohibitions will be set up. That is all.'

Few people have such clarity of insight into processes in which their lives are caught up; particularly when the Western way of life is presented as liberation, and its pervasive iconography of wealth, tolerance and ease is so ubiquitous and insistent.

Some of those who have actually lived outside India have another story to tell, one which certainly tempers the uncritical enthusiasm which many gay-identified men, and those who have the possibility of 'going out', take care to cultivate.

Karim lived in Toronto for four years in the 1970s. 'I was at the university doing a Ph.D. Naturally, I wanted to sample the gay bars, which I found astonishing in both the range and diversity of what they offered. But I had been there for just one month when the bar I was in happened to be raided. About one hundred people were arrested, and I was among them. I was released on bail as a foreigner and, although I remained in Toronto some years after that, it had still not come to court by the time I was to leave. So I left, technically still on bail, and therefore I was actually breaking the terms of my bail. My lawyer said to me, "Come back to Canada, and if you are arrested, I will come and bail you out at once." It was for me a traumatising experience in the land of freedom. That was in 1977.'

An architect and writer settled in London had a brutal experience of racism after two or three years. He was living modestly in the East End; going home late one night, walking through the tunnel under the Thames from Greenwich, he was attacked by some youths. They knocked him to the ground, beat and kicked him. His back was damaged, and the after-effects of this injury have troubled him ever since.

'But it is not so much the physical injuries as the psychological pain of it, and the constant reliving of that moment of knowing you are being followed, the faces of young men who do not know you, contorted with hate. As time has gone by, this has not diminished but has made me more frightened. I dare not go out alone after dark; and I sometimes find it quite difficult even in daylight. This is part of the price of leaving your home – a home where I was secure and the question of being accepted or not simply did not arise. On the other hand, my career has been here, and I've had a certain success. It leaves you torn, psychologically; the more so since my village and my home have been the source of my creative activity. It is very hard to quantify the negative elements and to set them against the advantages. I've also been able to live with my friend here in reasonable peace and acceptance. Whether it is worth it or not, it is quite difficult to decide; it is certainly more finely balanced than those who think that the West is Eldorado would have you believe.'

Karim says, 'Before I went to Canada, I had had a limited number of relationships with men in India. But the shortage of numbers was balanced by the intensity of the relationships. We built friendships that lasted and have continued until today. In Canada, I was shocked by the casualness of it all: the ease and abundance of partners, but also the readiness with which people discard and forget each other.

'It is now getting like this in India. What we saw in North America in the 1970s is being repeated here. Partly, this is a consequence of modernisation, as the coming of gay identity displaces other aspects of identity. Where sex is easily available, friendships do not flourish with the same depth of commitment. Sex, and the accompanying relationship, become more functional; although, of course, I'm aware that profound lifetime parnerships also flourish in the West.'

Sachin, a medical student who has relatives in the US, says he would like to live in the West. 'There I would be more free. Of course, I know that there are two sides to these things. In India, I must do many things for my parents, for the sake of duty. This teaches unselfishness. In the West, where you can do what you want, people are encouraged to shed responsibility and to think only of themselves. People become greedy and selfish. It is painful to be forced, out of love, to act out what to you are falsehoods; but at least you are doing it out of affection and love. It isn't all coercion, and you have the satisfaction of knowing you have placed other people's needs before your own. Having said that, I would still like to study in Cambridge or London.'

Rajan is thirty and works for a financial services company. He says, 'I expect to marry, but my first preference is for men. It is difficult for a woman in India if her husband likes men. I hope to find someone who is educated and who will understand, but I do not know if that is possible. In that case, concealment will be necessary, not only for the sake of the self-respect of my wife and myself, but also because of the family reputation. It is a great pity that women have no power in these matters. If she learns that her husband has sex with men, what will this do to her? How will she live with it? It will only disturb her expectations as wife and mother, without offering her any alternative but to sit at home brooding on what will seem to her a tragedy.

'This is now changing, slowly, even in India. It will change. Slowly this knowledge is coming. This is something that comes with modernisation, as society evolves. But it will be a long time before traditional attitudes are transformed. It will probably not come in my lifetime, so I will not benefit from it. But you cannot open up a country to the world as India is now opening up and try to resist the cultural influences that come with liberalisation. Consumerism changes people's whole concept of life purposes: you cannot preach spending and spending without also kindling people's appetites for other things. It is foolish and naïve to imagine that people will be satisfied only with a new washing machine or refrigerator. These things only free human energies that long to go off in search of other things.'

Ram Singh, an airman from Rajasthan, observes, 'If homosexuality becomes too open, the fundamentalists will make an issue of it. They will blame the West for corrupting Indian youth. But it is in our culture, in our past. It has been denied. It happens, plenty, but it is not to be discussed or talked of in any way. This is hypocrisy. There was one chief minister in Orissa, he used to bring boys from the village to his house in Delhi to work for him. People did not think of such a thing. It happens here because it is not openly in the experience of most people. To them, if they hear of it, it is something that happens elsewhere, abroad, in the West. If two young men are hanging on each other's necks, this is regarded as ordinary, nothing unusual; no one would ever imagine they might do anything together. If that thought was to be placed in their mind, people would be shocked and horrified, not least the young men themselves; and then all that sweet demonstrative friendship would cease. I wouldn't want that to happen under the banner of liberation; because for many people it would be the opposite of liberation.

'I've had much experience of abstinence, and not from choice. I do not believe that having relationships with men should be an offence. How can I think that? This is a cruel world, and when people give each other some comfort, whoever they are, it is not the work of government to stop it. In all fairness, of course, they don't. The statute against homosexuality is not often used; but the fact that it exists is an affront to human friendship and tenderness. It will change, but slowly. I am a supporter of the BJP, but not of the fundamentalists. The BJP are disciplined, and this is what India lacks.'

These conflicts, which create uncertainty and anguish in the lives of individuals, are also reflections of a wider and deeper social and economic split in India. In the public arena, it is taken as a foregone conclusion that the forces of 'globalisation', the exigencies of forms of modernisation, that are indistinguishable from the acceptance of Western values, must win; that their victory is inevitable obscures and makes invisible many of the objections, as well as the resistances, of those people who see and bear the untold, measureless human costs of such battles.

Shortly after working on this book, I was in Malaysia, where there is also an Article Three hundred and seventy-seven of the Penal Code in which the prohibition upon 'acts against the order of nature' is also enshrined. It is clear that this is part of the same gift from Britain to its former subject peoples. The builders of empire obviously had an off-the-peg penal code which they applied without taking any account of the values, traditions or morals of the culture which they had laid under subjection. It resembles contemporary accounts of the work of the International Monetary Fund, which has applied a blueprint for 'structural adjustment' to a great variety of countries, without any reference to the prevailing conditions or circumstances within the country in question. It is only that the operations of dominance change from age to age and now occur in different realms of experience. The continuities are unmistakable.

X

It cannot be stated too strongly that the conflict between modernisation and tradition is not just a question of ideas: the battle is played out in people's lives and at the deepest level. No one is exempt from the reshaping of sensibility, changes in the way we feel about each other, and the effect this has on our attempts to make sense of, and give meaning to, our deepest relationships.

I have known Sabhu for seven years. I met him when I went into the shop where he was working to get some trousers made. He was very friendly, and I was perhaps the first foreigner he had met. His was one of the first Indian houses I ever visited in Delhi. On the day my mother died and I had to leave suddenly, he was very attentive and kind, and stayed with me until it was time for me to go; he is a good friend. A devout Hindu, he is both a bearer of traditional values and an eager absorber of certain aspects of Western sensibility, its fashions and music especially. He is now twenty-nine, handsome, fleshy, running now, after six years of marriage, slightly to fat. He lives in east Delhi in a small brick apartment constructed by the Delhi Development Authority. His parents, his sister and her husband and child also live in the three-roomed flat. It is noisy and crowded; a small black-and-white TV plays all the time, so that conversation is often reduced to a competitive shouting.

Sabhu is sexually very active. He likes women and is also attracted to men, although he never talks about this. He enjoys being both the active and passive partner. He sometimes refers to men he has sex with as his 'underwear friends', meaning they will exchange and wear each other's underpants.

He is from a Kshatriya family, does daily puja, goes to the temple regularly and is always taking time from work to go on pilgrimages to Rishikesh, Hardwar, Varanasi. He is a strong supporter of the Bharatiya Janata Party and speaks virtually no English. He is sociable, warm and charming.

He is also impulsive and dominated by whim, easily distracted, but loyal, generous and affectionate. He does not spend a great deal of time at home. Like a man in the Victorian working class in Britain, he seeks his pleasures and relaxations outside the home and considers the raising of children to be 'women's work', no concern of his except when they need to be chastised for doing something wrong. One year, I spent every evening for a week with Sabhu visiting the various Dassehra Ramlila plays in different parts of the city. Sabhu loves play-acting, dressing up; and he was fascinated by the young men dressed up in the female roles.

Sabhu knows hundreds of people in Delhi, and wherever he goes in the city, 'friends' are always greeting him, asking him where he is going, which Hindi film he has seen, what he thinks of the cricket or hockey team, inviting him for a tea, a coffee, a cold drink, a beer. Most of these friends have no idea of his driven sexual nature; and indeed, he himself seems unconcerned about it most of the time. Certain elements of his life simply coexist. They do not need to be accounted for or explained away. They are all part of his inner self and that is the obvious integrating factor. Each experience and each need is a different aspect of his truth, and its place in the larger scheme of things requires no justification.

Sabhu is easily bored. He is hyperactive, always going to this party, that marriage of a friend, rushing across Delhi to meet someone who, as often as not, is not there. He works in a tailor's shop in a shopping centre on Mahatma Gandhi Road, an energetic and persuasive salesman earning three thousand rupees a month, which with commission reaches around four thousand five hundred rupees. He likes to dress fashionably and presently wears tight jeans, loose silk shirts, high-heeled cowboy-style boots, belts with elaborate buckles. One evening I went with him to a bar, where he drank too much. Then we went to a restaurant, where he ate one meal and then another. Afterwards he was sick.

Sabhu does not acknowledge limits. His life spills readily into what Westerners certainly regard as other people's spaces. He goes from person to person, looking for distraction, amusement. He will not wear a condom when he has sex because, he says, it spoils the pleasure.

Sabhu is happy to talk about the women in his life. He readily acknowledges that he has a girlfriend, with whom he is going away for a few days to one of the holy cities at the source of the Ganges. Sometimes he will go to GB Road and pay a sex worker, and he talks openly about his 'fucking programme'. He is eager to involve his friends in his excursions around the city looking for sex with women. He does not, however, show the same frankness when it comes to his sexual involvement with men, which is certainly far more extensive than any other aspect of his extramarital relationships. On the only occasion when I asked him if he likes sex with men, he said, *'Mujhe achcha nahin lagta'* (I don't like it). He says he thinks homosex is just for men who cannot get women. On the other hand, whenever I have seen him in the various cruising grounds in Delhi, he grins and says hello, as though he just happened to be passing through.

Integration through silence: Sabhu does not appear to be disturbed by the demands of his sexuality; only the frenzy of activity suggests that it may well be less easily accommodated in his life than he would like to believe. Suresh, by contrast, actually articulates very well the integration of his own ambiguous sexuality, so that he is at ease with its complementarity and does not feel his attraction to both women and men as conflict.

Suresh is in his forties, a widower with two children. He speaks beautifully about integration. One day, we sat overlooking the deep ruins at Hauz Khas, a day of wonderfully clear sunlight and lengthening September shadows, the sandstone red-gold in the afternoon sun. Suresh said that he has always been aware of the multiple identities which constitute his sense of self: 'son, husband, father, engineer, Hindu, Hindi and English speaker, lover, friend. These have coexisted, not all necessarily at the same time, and not always without conflict, but certainly without exclusiveness and without encroaching too much upon each other.

'I will say that the element that involves the attraction to men has always been the most difficult aspect of my being to accommodate. It sometimes seemed that there was not quite enough space for it in the crowded identities of my inner being, this meeting place where the different parts of myself come together.

'In my early twenties I went to Japan and was taken to the bars where gay men meet. As soon as I realised such places existed, I had a huge sense of excitement and relief. For a time I felt I was another person: not simply that there was at last room for another facet of my being, but space for someone else. I glimpsed what the thing we now call the politics of identity might be. I was away from home. No one knew me. I had temporarily shed – or at least stored away – the other main components of my identity. And I enjoyed it. I had a good time. But, being young, I didn't bother to set down deep roots; I had lots of experience, met many people, but didn't really make lasting friendships.

'When I returned to India, it was time to get married. I did what was expected, and that area of my life somehow returned to the dark-ness, or at least the shadows. I found my life as husband and father very fulfilling. It wasn't until after the death of my wife – and a long time after, when the grief at her loss had become less intense – that this other part of my self came out of hiding. When I could bear to start thinking about a new relationship, I knew that such a relationship would be with a man. Although I haven't yet found it, I now know that when I do, this will not be something extraneous to me; it won't be parenthesised, as it was when I was young in Japan. It will be part of that same, inner, harmonious throng of identities which occupy my inner world and live together there.

'The difference, I think, is this: when I was young, the wildness of sexual discovery in Japan, the promiscuity of the gay world, the ready availability of sexual encounters which had no consequences and no tomorrows, seemed to threaten the disintegration of the other aspects of my life, the rootedness and belonging of being a north Indian and Hindu. Now, the acceptance of same-sex relationships is a force for integration, a sign of completeness and wholeness: it doesn't threaten to overwhelm or crowd out the rest.'

During my stay in Delhi late in 1997, I found myself caught up in precisely this struggle between the forces of tradition and those of the market, in a way that I could never have foreseen. It made me feel, quite simply, that I was on the wrong side.

The cause of the dispute came from the actions of the Nai Azadi Bachao Andolan, the New Freedom Movement of India, a small but well-organised group of people dedicated to the preservation and enhancement of India's independence. Until this time, I had regarded them as valued friends and allies in the struggle against economic, cultural and political domination in India by the industrial powers and the Western financial and economic institutions. A liberalisation that erases indigenous industry, a deregulation that has introduced a voracious consumerism, a modernisation that creates a parody of Western society for the privileged, but without any of its amenities of basic welfare, controls on the exploitation of labour, proper health care, adequate nutrition and safe drinking water are all signs of a profound sickness at the heart of the developmental project.

But the Nai Azadi Bachao Andolan goes further in its distaste for Western influence. It obtained a court order requiring people to black out the offending portions of film posters which displayed portraits of underclad women. Then it took out a prosecution against two radio programmes broadcast by the All-India Radio, which featured phone-ins on homosexuality and divorce. These were sponsored by Population Services International and the Marie Stopes Clinic and were designed to offer factual information to people troubled by their sexuality or unhappy in their marriage. The programmes opened a serious discussion about the nature of human sexuality. The Andolan found them obscene and decided that they 'flouted moral standards'.

This is part of its wider critique of baleful Western influence, of which even the mention of such things appears to be a sinister symptom; even though the makers of the programmes were concerned to lessen ignorance about sex and human relationships and to deal openly with problems that trouble and inflict unnecessary suffering on millions of people in India. The Andolan was unable, it seemed to me, to distinguish between an educational project, on the one hand, and the exploitation of sex for commercial purposes, on the other. It was safeguarding a curious kind of liberty that wished to perpetuate ignorance rather than knowledge, a strange form of freedom that believes sex is somehow un-Indian, treating the people of India like children, who must not be exposed to discussions about homosexuality, extramarital affairs or rape because they cannot be trusted to make up their own minds on these subjects.

Whatever idea the Andolan may entertain about the sexual purity of Indians, statistics tell a different, and an alarming, story. According to figures from the Ministry of Health, more than 40 million cases of sexually transmitted diseases are reported annually. It is now widely recognised that HIV and AIDS will affect more people in India than in any other country in the world. It is an open secret that the sex industry in India is one of the most highly organised and ruthless in the world, with scores of thousands of women in the brothels of Delhi, Chennai, Calcutta, Mumbai and all the other major cities, as well as in all the towns through which trucks pass on the main highways. The traffic in women and girls from Nepal, from tribal areas and from the northeast is big business. The existence of tens of millions of migrants in India, mostly lone men who must travel far from home in search of a meagre and often inadequate livelihood, creates a growing demand for sexual services, a demand which is always going to be supplied.

It is hard to imagine how, by driving such issues further underground, India will be in a position to combat the terrible human tragedies which such statistics suggest lie in wait for its people. The sanctity of marriage is scarcely going to be furthered by policies of denial, concealment and unknowing. These preservers of Indian freedom are in fact seeking to impose yet another ideology upon the people: not market liberalisation, not state socialism, but a curious and archaic form of Victorian morality.

Here is the supreme irony: while defending their country against neo-colonialism, they are responding with the kind of prudery, puritanism and hypocrisy that have little to do with Indian tradition and everything to do with the legacy of colonial rule. In other words, they are reverting to an older form of the colonialism they repudiate in order to resist a newer one.

As we know, Indian culture has traditionally celebrated diverse sexualities: temple carvings at Khajahuro, Konark and elsewhere testify to great ingenuity and an exuberant delight in multiple sexualities and the pleasures of the body. The fact that I and my friends, as fourteen-year-olds in our school in the English Midlands, passed to and fro under our desks copies of the Kamasutra scarcely suggests a culture that has traditionally sought to control human sexuality, its diversity and inventiveness of expression. The proscriptions and denials are essentially a product of the nineteenth century, and that means the Raj. It is another paradox that while Article Three Hundred and seventy-seven still remains in force, the British themselves have long since seen fit to abandon such legislation for their own people.

The attack on homosexuality is another example of an illiberal and uncharitable response to actually existing humanity by those who call themselves humanitarians.

As the testimonies of the men in this book make clear, those who are married yet still have sex with men risk carrying back HIV to their wives and unborn children. Without a far more realistic programme of education than anything at present in place, lakhs of women and children will bear the brunt of an official negligence which the guardians of India's freedom seem to want to institutionalise as a matter of high principle.

But there is worse. To say that homosexuality is a foreign phenomenon, a manifestation of Western colonialism and decadence, exhibits a profound misundersanding of the nature of human sexuality. Freedom in the hands of those who defend this particular and diminished version will swiftly become something else. After all, it was part of Hitler's grisly project to send sexual deviants, along with Jews, gypsies and others he considered to be subhumans, to the gas chambers. Strange allies. Strange freedoms. Homosexuality – however it may be constructed and in whatever form it may express itself – exists in all cultures and all societies. To seek to 'stamp out' something so ineradicable will finish up in a programme of mass persecution.

The effect of prosecuting the makers of such programmes is anti-woman as well as anti-gay. For to transform the sanctity of the family into an ideology is to condemn millions of women to joyless, unloving and sometimes brutal marriages. We have only to look at the incidence of atrocities against women within the family to realise that the number of cases that come to public attention represent only a fragment of the reality. Why would anyone want to perpetuate against women forms of a prejudice that sees them as subordinate creatures, guarantors of male supremacy, no matter what violence it does to them? The version of a tradition that elevates 'woman' in the abstract has a darker side. And if women really get such a good deal out of Indian tradition, why is the ratio of women to men at an historic low?

Surely anyone wishing to safeguard the, alas, already compromised freedom of India would not base defence of its freedoms on something so illiberal, inhumane and unkind. Far from carrying out its expressed intentions, the Andolan only threatens to drive India deeper into the darkness of ignorance, prejudice and denial. And of these India has already surely had enough.

XI

The argument against such a policy of denial seems to me overwhelming. Even though a culturally appropriate response – targeting the sexual behaviour of men rather than Western categories of identity – in the fight against AIDS may be more difficult than the present policy, which consists principally of an unhappy mixture of exhortation and vagueness, denial makes this arduous work even more impossible, particularly when its object is as amorphous and shifting as the fluid sexuality of so many of the men I met in the Park – men who were for the most part ordinary people, with conventional families, doing humdrum work.

Amongst these men, there is, of course, a high level of risky behaviour, partly as a result of misunderstanding the danger to health posed by unprotected sex. 'With men, sex is easy,' affirms Tushar. 'It is safe, there is no problem. It is quick and soon finished. There is no consequence. Men are clean. I would not go to prostitutes.'

One man, a *thikedar* (contractor of labour) who had travelled several hundred miles to Delhi precisely for sex, said that he did not use any precautions: 'Men are safe. You cannot catch sexual diseases from men. I do not use any condom. You do not need to take precautions.'

Raju, who has been in the army for six months, fucks his superior officer. They do not use a condom because, says Raju, the officer tells him it is safe between men. AIDS comes only from vaginal sex.

Pradeep, thirty-eight, has been in the central reserve police force for the past six years. He discovered that he liked sex with men only after he joined the force. Until that time he had had sex only with his wife, whom he married when he was twenty-three. He was initiated by a younger man, who asked him to penetrate him. Pradeep likes to be in the company of men and prefers it to domestic life. He enjoys penetrating men because, he says, the anus is tighter than the vagina, and he finds this gives a more pleasurable sensation. He has tried to use a condom, but rejected it because this interferes with the pleasure.

Mahesh, twenty, is a passive partner for men who will pay for sex. Although he sees himself as a professional, in practice he has little control over the pay he gets. If the man decides not to pay afterwards, there is nothing he can do about it. On the other hand, some are generous, and on occasion he can make two hundred rupees a day. Mahesh knows of the danger of AIDS, but if his clients will not wear a condom, he cannot compel them. 'What to do? I have to live. If I get AIDS, this will not be tomorrow; but if I don't eat for a week, I'll be dead.'

Gurjinder, forty, does not have friendships with the men he has sex with in the Park. He has reduced his sexual need to simple discharge. He makes sure his feelings remain with his wife and family. He comes to the Park every ten to fifteen days. He knows that sex with strangers can be risky. He says he once had some persistent sores around the genitals, but went to a private sex doctor in Patelnagar, who gave him some ointment; after a few months, the lesions went away.

Jitender, a Delhi policeman, says he has sex with men, 'because I am far from home'. He misses the comforts of the family and the affection of his wife. He is staying in a police barracks, where they sleep thirty or forty to a room. He says that there is never any sexual contact between the men in the barracks, but he knows of others who enjoy when they get the opportunity. Jitender is thirty, and he likes older men. He always takes the active role. He has never heard the word *gay*. He comes here only for relief. He does not use a condom, because this interferes with the enjoyment. Even so, he has heard people talk about the risks of unprotected sex. He doesn't believe it. I ask, 'What if you take this back home to your wife?' He shrugs and says, 'Sex with men is safe.' He has heard that AIDS is something you get from female prostitutes, but since he never does that, he has no fear.

His friend joins us as we sit on the bench under the eucalyptus tree. He hears us talking about condoms and says that he knows of the work of NAZ, whose outreach workers have been visiting the Park, talking of safe sex and distributing condoms. This man also says that he will not wear a condom. He says that to avoid AIDS and other sexually transmitted diseases, he takes some Ayurvedic pills which, he is convinced, render him immune to exposure to all STDs.

When I meet Sudhir he is just about to go home to Lucknow for a week's holiday. This is the first time in several weeks that he has come to the Park to look for sex, in which he is the active partner. He has been ill with fever, was in hospital for a fortnight and has not yet returned to his work as a tailor. He is feeling weak, has a bad cough and has lost a lot of weight. Occasionally he has coughed blood. He is frightened and asks if I am a doctor. I give him the address and telephone number of the doctor who is working for NAZ. Later, when I make enquiries, I find that he has made no contact with him.

Rawat, thirty-two, came into the Park for the first time only a year ago. It was a hot night, and he came to cool down. A man sat next to him on a bench and asked him if he wanted to fuck him. 'I said no, but my heart said yes. I was no longer in control of myself. I went with him, not knowing what would happen. I had never looked at a man's backside before, and I had never thought about men in that way. I became very excited by the tightness of a man's arse. I used saliva to lubricate my cock. A woman is this shape [he makes an oval with his hands] and loose, but a man is this shape [he makes a circle with thumb and forefinger] and tight, which gives a better feeling. I know it is a risk to do like that, but when I found out that this was possible, I started to think about it all the time. I use Vaseline to make it easier. One time I had some rash on my penis after sex. I do not know what it was, but it was very irritating and inflamed. I mixed some salt with masala and rubbed it on. This was very painful, but it went away. I always wash thoroughly afterwards.'

There is an even more fundamental problem, and that is in defining precisely what constitutes sex. For some time, I was puzzled by the assertions of men whom I had seen regularly in the Park that they had never had sex. This seemed at first to be only a more flagrant kind of denial. But for many, 'sex' means vaginal intercourse with a woman. Whatever they did with men did not count; indeed, it did not even constitute sexual activity at all. It became clear that 'play' or 'fun' belonged to a quite separate order of experience; this suggested a degree of dissociation which I had not believed possible.

Balu, a dark-skinned, tall young man, says he is eighteen but looks older. Today, he has been sleeping on a bench in the Park and is just waking up. It is three o'clock in the afternoon. His jeans are dirty, his shoes scuffed, his hair greasy and he exudes an air of neglect. He left home at thirteen and worked in Delhi as a tea boy, then on a snack stall, then as a security guard. He left this last job six months ago when he discovered there was money to be made in the Park. Balu does not like staying in the room he rents, and he uses every opportunity to be out and looking for clients. Even that can be tedious. Balu waits for them to approach him. He does not like the ceaseless patrolling of the *khotis*, who walk up and down and chase after every new man who comes into the Park.

'I do not like sex with men, but it is easier to make a living than being a security guard. Sometimes the men will not wear a condom, but I always carry some with me. But I need money, so I don't think about it if they say no; the future doesn't exist in this game not even tomorrow. Today I've got nothing.' He yawns, tousled, dishevelled. 'But that doesn't matter,' he grins. 'Things get better after dark.'

Balu says if he could choose work, he would like to get service in a private house. 'But I don't know how to cook.' He has no qualifications, having left school at twelve.

Two of his friends join him. One says he is a carpenter, the other admits he has no other means of livelihood than sex in the Park. As darkness falls, they make their way to the bus stand, which is in front of the Park and at the corner of a busy junction. Here, people wait for inter-state buses, going north and west out of Delhi. The traffic is so busy that at certain times of day it is impossible to cross the road. It is dusty and noisy, with the incessant honking of buses, trucks, Tempos, two-wheelers and cycles; crowds of people with cases, holdalls, trunks and bundles of goods; together with vendors of peanuts, *channa*, oranges, *poori bhaji* and soft drinks.

The shifting population around the bus stand serves as a kind of camouflage for the young men soliciting, if that is the right word. For the most part, they remain still, and contact is made by a glance, an inclination of the head, the smallest movement, undetectable to outsiders. In any case, most people are too busy making sure they get their bus, anxiously scanning each new arrival and reading its destination, asking others if this one is indeed going to Jaipur. Only after standing

167

for some time you become aware of those who are not moving; the men casually wandering up and down, briefly scrutinising the boys in the bus shelter or under the lamplight.

This also goes on throughout the day, but since there are quite a lot of traffic police and there is always a police presence, this can be a little risky; particularly if the boys wear more fashionable or showy clothes than most of the travellers, who are, on the whole, shabby or at least in everyday wear.

After dark, business becomes much more brisk. Balu says that even if there are no clients in the Park during daylight hours, there is always the evening, when he can earn twice as much. This is why he is unhurried and relaxed in the daytime. He will be picked up at the bus stand, and they will go into the Park. Although the main gate is closed at sunset, there are many gaps in the wall and in the railings; and in places, holes have been made in the brick walls, large enough for people to pass through. In any case, the gate at the side of the Park remains open, with its rusting painted metal sign saying Kitchener Lake.

I ask the three young men what will happen if they ask their clients to use a condom. 'Maybe. If they are educated people, sometimes they have a condom. If not, they will not think of it. If we ask them, they will find somebody else. Look [he indicates with a hand the throng around the bus stand].' There must be twenty or thirty young men, loitering, challenging the glances of passers-by. Some older men pause, linger. Balu sets off, and one of the men follows him. As they proceed down the road, the client catches up with him, so that it looks as if they have been walking along together all the time.

The first time Abhijit had sex with a man, he was coming out of work late one night and was picked up by a boy, who took him to some waste jungle land behind the hotel where he works. When he took out his cock, the boy – who was a Muslim – was very shocked, because Abhijit had not cleaned beneath the foreskin. The boy said it was very smelly and would only masturbate. 'He told me he likes to suck, but he wouldn't do that. I was very upset, because to be told you are dirty is humiliating, and if he is a Muslim, it only makes it worse. I think it was true. I never had sex with anyone before. I did not think my cock would be dirty. I always take a bath twice a day, but I never thought I ought to wash beneath the skin. Now I wash there every day, and now no one says that to me.'

Man Singh, who has been in the army for fifteen years, says: 'I came to know of sex with men only after joining the army. I heard men talking of going to houses where there are young girls to be had for money. A friend told me that sex here [in the Park] is free. He said, 'There is only one small problem – it is all between men." I could not believe it. At first I did not pay much attention to what he said. But it sat in my mind for a long time. One day, I thought I would see what is happening here. Since then, I come two or three times in a month. I like to be sucked or to fuck. I do not like kissing, and I will not let anyone penetrate me. I do not want to touch another man, only his backside. I do not care to see his cock. Like that, it is secure. There is no risk. I am a man. I want discharge only.' A majority of the men who call themselves active have no interest in the genitals of the partner.

Premchand, twenty-three, 'I only want to kiss and sleep with a man. Nothing else. I do not like the *pani* to come out. It is dirty, and I find it disgusting. It makes you weak and it also affects your intelligence. If you do it with your hand, it makes your penis lose its shape.'

Rajinder, twenty-two, says the opposite. He likes to have men come in his mouth or in his backside. He says, 'It makes you stronger. If you swallow, it feeds the life-force. Especially if he is a real man, you get some of his strength.'

Dhirendra, an army man in his mid thirties, says: 'When I have free time, I come to Dhaula Kuan to look for sex. I was married, and I have one son. My wife died of cancer four years ago. My son stays with my parents in the village. Only since she died, I look for sex with men. I like men. I like to fuck, because it is tighter than a woman's body. I am looking for company, for friends. Sex is just for release. The army is a cold place. There is no comfort there. I use a condom now. I used not to, but sometimes you can catch things if you put your penis in the backside of a stranger. I had a bad-smelling discharge. I went to a pharmacy and told them I had a chest infection and I needed strong antibiotics. That cleared it up. The second time I had to get two lots of medicine before it went away.'

Among the accounts of their sexual activity, there appeared many myths and many practices that are dangerous and pose great risks to health. Similarly, some of the remedies against STDs were highly unorthodox and unreliable.

It is widely believed that HIV occurs only in the West, specifically in the United States. This was asserted by some men as a matter of literal truth. 'I don't think about AIDS, because I have never been with a Westerner,' said one man. Another thought it was a 'disease of Africans'.

It is also believed that HIV can only be transmitted through vaginal sex. Anal sex is declared to be 'safe'. This conveniently blames women for transmission of the virus and was quoted by seven men (9 per cent) as a reason for not visiting female sex workers.

Some men claimed that HIV/AIDS is curable. The belief that sex with a virgin is a cure for venereal disease is of great antiquity and occurs across cultures; it is only a short leap to transfer this to more recent scourges. Some also believe that sex with an animal – a dog or a monkey, for example – 'cures' all such evils. One visitor from Bangladesh had heard people in Dhaka say that sex with an ugly woman is also a cure.

The conviction that anal sex is safe is reinforced by a belief that to receive the semen of another male strengthens you. This is connected with the Hindu belief that the conservation of semen makes men stronger and that this vital force is stored in the crown of the head. The high value traditionally accorded to sexual abstinence comes from this belief, as does the assertion that too frequent ejaculation weakens the body. This also leads to much of the negative mythology concerning masturbation: it leads to a distortion of the shape of the penis; it makes the penis turn black; you will eventually ejaculate blood; it damages brain activity. All of these were spoken as a matter of solemn truth.

Some of the *khotis* wash out their anus with Dettol after having sex. One man thought this would protect him against HIV. Others cited the use of lemon juice, masala and even *agarbatti* [incense-stick] smoke. Some thought there were Ayurvedic or alternative medicines, herbal infusions and pastes which were efficacious against STDs. Piles and bleeding are common afflictions. One man had cut out his piles with an open razor. Cures for warts, gonorrhoea and other sexually transmitted diseases indicated the power of superstition, in relation both to traditional specifics and to Western proprietary medicines and disinfectants.

It is clear that many *khotis* – with their imitative feminised behaviour (which is also a way of signalling to prospective partners that they are passive) – have also internalised the low esteem in which women are held in India. Powerless and fatalistic, for many of the professional *khotis*, livelihood must take precedence over life itself. The only protection they have against the invisible threat of HIV/AIDS lies in weaving an extraordinary tissue of belief which they wrap around themselves, an invisible mantle to ward off evils that are all too real.

Such beliefs are symbolic, the only shelter of the powerless. They tell us more about the nature of faith – in any setting, in any environment, in any society – than about the safety of those whose lives are informed by it. To listen to this profound expression of faith is like being present at the formulation of a religious conviction. The need to believe in their immunity is a more powerful factor in their lives than the ability to do anything about it.

It is clear, then, that there are many untreated sexually transmitted diseases, many unresolved sexual problems and many confusions in terms of sexual orientation and identity. An impression of powerlessness and subordination.

However, to talk to people as individuals is one thing, but to meet them collectively is quite a different order of experience. You soon learn that there are networks, support groups and relationships that extend far beyond the accounts given in individual interviews.

For one thing, the Park itself takes on the characteristics of a location apart, in which different group identities are assumed, elective changes of role can occur: a sense of magical possibilities, a transformation of the context of Delhi life with its domination by family, marriage and children. It is a kind of natural drop-in centre, a haven and refuge from the socially constructed duties of husbands, sons and fathers, the site of a holiday from heterosexuality to which many come regularly, especially on Sundays.

Kamaluddin is a young man of twenty-three who comes from Nainital. He works in a private school as a *chaprasi*, a kind of helper, whose duties include ringing the bell at the end of each lesson, maintaining the stock of materials for the teachers and doing odd jobs around the school. He earns Rs 1500 a month. Kamal loves dancing, which he does well, giving impromptu performances in the Park. He will take a chiffon scarf and turn it into a living thing, gyrating and turning, making all the eye and hand movements familiar from both Hindi films and classical dance.

But sex is his profession, his hobby and his obsession. He likes to suck and is happy to be a passive partner, and he augments his income at the same time. He comes to the Park most afternoons when school is finished, at weekends and during holidays. Even when he makes no money, he is exuberant and uninhibited: he will sit with his head in someone's lap or hanging on the neck of a friend, sticking out his tongue or moving his hips in movements suggestive of sexual activity. Occasionally, strangers in the Park – couples or people using the Park as a short cut from the village to the main road – stop to look at him with curiosity. He remains cheerful and seductive under their astonished glace.

But once outside the Park, Kamaluddin is another person: subdued, correct, timid. The contrast is dramatic, a measure of the degree of liberation which this place represents.

But it remains precarious, even in this protected site. Suddenly, once more, the police are present. A corpulent officer in khaki, with red flashes on his uniform and a revolver in his holster, is patrolling the jungle paths. He walks stealthily and for a moment looks like a hunter – a man-having-sex-with-a-man-hunt. A senior officer is talking to a policeman in plain clothes, who has been acting as an *agent provocateur*, encouraging men to follow him into the bushes. In the jungle they round up and arrest a few *khotis* and their clients found with their pants down. They take a few of them to the police station.

Later, I meet Yusuf, who has moved on to another cruising ground. 'I guess I'll stay away for a few days,' he says. 'They must have spent their Diwali bonus already, or maybe the pay commission award they got this week has made them greedy. But what are they doing here, when there are buses in Delhi being bombed, when crime and robbery and murder are increasing all over the city? The traffic is in chaos, there is corruption in every department. A few men playing with each other in the Park isn't really so terrible, is it, that they have to come and do like this?'

The men who are penetrated take on a separate group identity, calling themselves *khotis*. The professionals, too, form a distinct group, although the groups overlap. Then there are the men who do not see themselves as desiring other men, but claim they are only seeking sexual discharge. These are called *giriyas* by the *khotis*. They tend to be alone or in twos and threes, certainly not the large groups which the *khotis* sometimes form. In addition, there are the men who admit that they *karta hain aur karvata hain*, that is, they are sometimes active, sometimes passive. Finally, there are gay-identified men who, as we have seen, tend to be Western-influenced, often English-speaking, mostly middle class and economically well off.

The strongest sense of group solidarity occurs between the *khotis* and many men who call themselves gay also meet, some as a gay support group, outside the Park.

The first time I saw the *khotis* as a group was on a Sunday afternoon. I was walking through the Park when suddenly, between a break in the red rocks – which are about three metres high – I saw twenty or thirty men. I was surprised and quite apprehensive. I thought at first they might be a gang; but then I could see that they were well dressed, and they looked more like members of a Sunday outing on a picnic. Closer still, they were exuberant and cheerful; they greeted me enthusiastically. One man said loudly, in a theatrical way, 'I have a problem. I need a big *likum*. Can you answer my problem?' As a group, they were confident and assertive, quite different from when you meet them individually and, more significantly, quite different from when they are outside the Park.

Part of the group strength and solidarity comes from this growing identification of themselves as *khotis*. Later, I sat with a group under the trees and talked about this emerging identity. On this occasion, there were two government servants, one employee of a private company, two dancers, one professional sex worker, an employee of Air India and a driver. When I asked the sex worker what his job was, the others laughed and replied for him, 'Only five rupees a suck.' When they are together, they say that they speak Farsi. Farsi is actually a metaphor for a private language that has evolved between them, which outsiders will not understand, in which key words are substituted for the Hindi equivalents. They gave me a lesson in Farsi; and they came up with a vocabulary:

ðungor:	policeman
likum:	cock
ðhurwana:	to penetrate
komer:	to suck

bottel:	backside
bittu:	hips
ðharki:	nipple
ðhumki:	cigarette
thipur:	money
bhapki:	tea
kilwa:	to drink alcohol
chilku:	circumcised

This is just a sample of the separate language; a phenomenon known to many oppressed or criminalised groups who wish to assert their identity, to keep secrets and maintain their apartness from the mainstream.

Three of this group were married, two with children. All insist that no one in their places of work and no one in their personal lives – apart from their acquaintances in the Park – knows anything about their sexual preferences. One of the married men says, 'I never think about being married until I get into bed at night.'

There is a highly theatrical element in acting out this rudimentary gay role. It is a stereotype, which nevertheless represents a kind of escape; whether or not it corresponds to their needs is less important than the fact that this alternative exists, a scenario is written which they know how to play out. It serves as a relief and an escape from the macho roles they must maintain in their daily public lives; and anything that represents something different from that form of play-acting – even if it is only another kind of play-acting – must be a liberation.

One young man said he would do anything to get out of India. He is unhappy that his own country cannot accommodate him and that the only way out is this brief moment of relaxation on Sunday afternoons. Some of the others also assert that 'going out', leaving the country, is an attractive idea. Others say that it is no use thinking of such things, because dreams of escape only undermine efforts to stay and fight for the great majority, who have no choice but to remain.

Someone shouts *'Dungor'* as a jeep passes between the red rocks, setting up a cloud of dust. Most of the *khotis* scatter. One young man remains seated and says to me, 'Do not move. What are we doing that we need to run away the minute the police appear?' In any case, it turns out this time to have been a false alarm, some officials, maybe government employees, who have come for a picnic in the Park. The dust settles, coating the leaves and flowers with a brownish film that dims the vibrancy of the colours.

The others return. 'Why did you run away?' I ask. 'We have good reason,' they say. 'We don't want to be robbed, beaten or fucked by the police. We don't want any of these things or any combination of them, including, on occasions, a mixture of all three.'

Some of the *khotis* have a regular *giriya*; this is not a term which the 'active' men attribute to themselves. One of the *khotis* is wearing *khadi* [homespun cloth]. He has pale-coloured skin and light brown-green eyes. He says, 'I am a housewife.' He lives with a man and says he is very happy. When the others discuss men, they do so like women, commiserating with each other over their thoughtlessness, selfishness and lack of delicacy. Their feminised behaviour is strangely familiar. They remind me of the women of my childhood, clustered around door-steps in the working-class street, sharing stories of the inconstancy, incomprehensibility and irresponsibility of their husbands.

Another Sunday, a few weeks later. The heat is overwhelming. Languor and exhaustion. We are sitting on the grass. People come and go in the group, always with an eye open for unattached men. Among the *khotis* on this day there is a man who sells clothes outside the Regal Cinema in Connaught Place, an employee of an electronics company, an importer of books from the West on management, a hotel worker, an engineer, a shop worker, a bus driver and a student. One man is in his fifties, with thin hennaed hair; the student is eighteen, with tight jeans and a gold ear-stud. Some are middle-aged men, the image of settled married life. Some wear flashy rings; others are without orna-ment. Here, those who choose to be can be outrageous, boisterous.

They can let go with confidence. 'Things will change,' they insist, 'although maybe not for twenty, thirty years.' They regret that there is no outlet in Delhi, no restaurant or club, no commercial place at any rate. For them, the Park represents 'a holiday from life'. It is, for those who are married, a day off from heterosexuality, a treasured interval in a life of concealment and denial. Although they expressed the conviction that attitudes in India would change, none felt it would be either wise or feasible to organise for the purpose. It seems to them to be inscribed in a future of progress and development, which will come as a consequence of India's opening up to the wider world.

The *giriyas* have their own means of self-protection, although, on the whole, there is not the same defensive and collective network that has evolved among those who are penetrated. For one thing, the active partners take consolation from a mainstream dogma of maleness, of being 'real men', which means they can dispense with the irrational prejudices of the *khotis*. It became clear from our conversations that those who *karte hain* have no subjective problems with sexual identity. Some articulated this: those who fuck are men, there is no ambiguity, no matter into whom they discharge. It is only the receiving vessel, as it were, who may need to interrogate himself on the nature of his sexuality.

One day, I sat for over an hour with Amal, a driver in the army. He is thirty-one, a handsome man, who was anxious to talk about his wife and new baby, his second child. He wanted to know if it was true that people in the West have sex out of marriage. This is something he would never do. He says Western ways are bad. One man should stay with one woman for life. He comes from a village near Ilahabad. He does not like the army, because it gives him no freedom. He wants to be back home with his family.

I saw him again a little later. He was cheerfully going into the jungle with one of the *khotis*. He greeted me warmly before disappearing into the functional invisibility of the jungle, the invisibility of a place abstracted from the familiar daily world, in which things that happen do not exist objectively, for they are not named. What people do can easily be integrated into a system of belief; yet if these actions are named, they take on a materiality which merely doing does not possess. '*Chod deta hum*,' said one man. I fuck, therefore I am a man, he was saying.

Many of the *giriyas* in the Park come from the cantonment area – army, air force, navy, police, border security force, reserve police force. It soon appears that most of the service personnel have at least been given realistic instruction. One army man said they were told that hygiene is second only to security. They have been lectured by senior officers on the need to use a condom in any physical relationship (gender of partner not specified) beyond that with their wives. The army camps are like much of Delhi – single sex labour camps, full of lone males, whose raw sexual energy prowls the city, almost like a physical presence. People cut off from family, village and home are bound to find such comforts as they can in the brief intervals from the discipline of work and the relief of the sleep of exhaustion. Since the whole developmental pattern of India has led to these single-sex communities of strangers, it only makes official denials and unknowing the more painful and the more dangerous.

I was talking about the issue of AIDS in India at a seminar at the Teen Murti library. Afterwards, I had a brief conversation with a historian, who told me I was 'an imperialist of compassion'. He said that this is all in the tradition of those missionaries of the Raj who came to save the souls of the people of India. 'You are trying to save us from ourselves, our own ignorance, our own backwardness. You will go back to Britain and confirm the stereotypes of India as being incapable of self-governance.'

Having been stung by this, I have to acknowledge it contains an element of truth. While the principal purpose of the West remains an extractive one in India, as elsewhere in the South (the flow of wealth in the world from poor to rich remains constant through time), nevertheless this process requires concealment. What better cover than the humanitarian impulse of all the charity, aid and bringers of assistance to countries on whose continuing poverty the edifice of affluence of a minority of the world is constructed?

Some Reflections

It is now widely recognised that there are other forms of male-to-male sex than those encoded in the Western version of being gay or bisexual, even though everywhere Western colonialism and influence have modified indigenous alternative sexualities. The survival of older patterns, however degraded, has been acknowledged in recent years, not least because Western models of AIDS prevention in the area of men's sexual behaviour have been shown to be inappropriate in India and elsewhere. Such a perception has emerged not from theory, but from the direct experience of those working in the field. The UNAIDS programme makes this explicit:

> Sexual identity is different from sexual behaviour. Many men who have sex with other men do not regard themselves as homosexual. In a number of societies, the way such men view their own sexual identity is determined by whether they are the insertive or receptive partner in anal sex. In these societies, many men who have sex with other men self-identify as completely heterosexual, on the grounds that they take an exclusively insertive role in such activities. Worldwide, a large percentage of MSM are married and have sex with women as well.

These remaining – if attenuated – diversities are at the core of this book. Although I have been concerned with only one area of behaviour – men who have sex with men – this raises many other unresolved questions. One of these is whether, with globalisation, there will be a convergence of cultural patterns of same-sex behaviour in the world; this would lead to a wider emergence in the South of lesbian and gay movements of the kind familiar in Europe and North America. Alternatively, it may be that globalisation itself calls forth the recovery and reassertion of half-effaced indigenous sexualities, even if, as a recent article in *New Left Review* claims, 'the idea of returning to a completely pre-colonial or non-Western sexuality is now everywhere utopian.'

The same article also stated, in a passage on the repression of lesbians and gays in the South:

> In general, those who repress Third World lesbians and gay men are one-sidedly selecting from and manipulating indigenous traditions. Anti-gay attitudes do not help to free Third World peoples from outside domination. Rather, they are a single aspect of their more general suffering under the 'New World Order' and the current global economic crisis. Newly arising gay and lesbian movements are an aspect of Third World peoples' efforts to reclaim and redefine their nations and cultures.

This is not necessarily true. For instance, in India an unofficial alliance between Gandhians and religious fundamentalists to prevent any discussion of same-sex relationships comes from a shared view that these represent the influence of a decadent West. Such a proscription depends for its legitimation upon an ancient tradition of *brahmacharya* [sexual continence], of continence and abstention. This, fused with colonial prohibitions upon such relationships, has left a lingering puritanical consensus of denial, which in turn has led to an official lack of will to confront some of the principal conduits whereby HIV/AIDS is spreading in India. Yet these movements are also, in other respects, unquestionably in the forefront of the fight against Western dominance. All living ideological struggles manipulate certain aspects of belief and culture at the expense of others; and these conflicting elements contend for supremacy.

Discussion around sexuality, of course, forms only one small part of a wider and deeper debate about globalisation and the sources of cultural and local resistance to its powerful compulsions. It seems, from the contemporary experience in India, that both acceptance of and resistance to globalisation and its consequences are occurring simultaneously. While the spread of market culture creates a class of people likely to react in much the same way as Western lesbians and gay men – even under the threat of continuing official and legal disapproval – at the same time, this very development also calls forth a desire on the part of a minority of lesbians and gays not to imitate the West, but to rediscover and revalidate traditions that had lapsed or gone underground as a result of colonial prohibitions. How far these are retrievable is debatable.

A new element is added to this debate by the fact that the universalising of the market economy and the consumer society remains unrealistic, indeed materially impossible, for a majority of people in the South. The question of what will happen to the poor under the impact of Western reforms, liberalisation, privatisations, and all the economic nostrums advocated by the Western financial institutions, governments of the G-7, the WTO and the transnationals remains unclear.

This has significant implications for the debate about same-sex relations: people can scarcely be expected to wait for the liberating potential of Western-style affluence to sanction their sexual behaviour. This version of lesbian and gay emancipation is simply not going to occur. Other forms of repressed or denied sexualities have already arisen; people will always create some space for themselves in however hostile an environment, as the testimony of the men here make clear.

There is certainly, from the Indian experience, a powerful correlation between market culture and gay-identity politics. This reaches only a small percentage of the people, although it is a very influential group, prominent in industry, in the media and communications. A pervasive iconography of Western luxury and affluence, and the lifestyles that accompany it, are likely to have a disproportionate influence upon the rest of the society.

The terrain on which the struggle is being waged is that of local, specific cultural characteristics: How far are these destined to be submerged by the spread of a global consumer culture? And to what extent may they be conserved, recuperated and reclaimed from the burden of colonialisms old and new? Will some fusion of both occur, unevenly perhaps, but in such a fashion as to give rise to new ways of being in the world, including new forms of sexual expression? (New forms that are, of course, also old forms, for there is no sexual orientation, no transgenderism or transvestism, no permutation of human sexualities that has not found some outlet, sanctioned by religion and custom or forbidden by morality and tradition, in all cultures, in one guise or another.)

Such debates are given an added poignancy by the fact that just as market culture appears to have achieved unchallengeable supremacy in the world, its very survival is in question. At the very moment when the world has been made safe for capitalism, it may be that capitalism – with its excessive abuse of resources, its voracious appetites and deregulation of the desires of five or six billion human beings – is no longer safe for the world. The possible terminal subversion of the resource base of the planet by this agent of liberation only poses further questions about the nature and direction of all attempts at human emancipation.

These are discussions which do not present themselves overtly here; but they hover, spectral, insistent, menacing, around all the debates about survival. The necessary symbiosis of people and planet is threatened by a form of development where livelihood is so often at war with life, and daily survival is at odds with the longer-term preservation of a resource base upon which all social and economic systems and the relationships within them, ultimately depend.

Perhaps one of the most optimistic things we can say is that, despite the growing market in young women – and men – in the global sex trade, nevertheless, for the great majority of human beings, sexual exchange remains a free gift, an expression of uncoerced reciprocality and desire. As such, it does not use up scarce resources; it represents one of the great reservoirs of human energy which replenishes itself freely and constantly; it is both costless and pleasurable, no matter what social and religious sanctions might seek to limit and direct its expression.

Of course, the threat of HIV, and the ravages that have already occurred in some parts of the world, demand even greater efforts of control and prevention in order to conserve and to enhance this precious free gift. To this end, a more imaginative and creative understanding of actually existing human sexualities is vital. I offer this book, with gratitude and affection, to the workers of NAZ India in New Delhi, in the hope that their work will enhance the understanding and tolerance of yet another dimension of the diversity that is India.